Starting and Succeeding
In Your Own
Small Business

Starting and Succeeding In Your Own Small Business

by
Louis L. Allen
President of the Chase Manhattan Capital Corporation

Foreword by
Frank L. Tucker
Professor, Harvard Business School

Introduction by
Wilford L. White
Former Director, Division of Management Assistance, Small Business Administration

Publishers   GROSSET & DUNLAP   *New York*

© 1968 by Louis L. Allen
Library of Congress Catalog Card Number: 67-14763
All rights reserved.
Published simultaneously in Canada.
ISBN: 0-448-01177-8
1977 Printing

Printed in the United States of America

I once made a bet that every successful small businessman had received support and encouragement at home, that his family was very much involved in his small business and that, if asked, the small businessman would affirm it. I lost the bet because I wagered with a friend who loves to make me lose; he found a successful small businessman who was an orphan and a bachelor. Well, that's the trouble with making a bet.

Most small businessmen (to satisfy the doubting Thomases) must have a family life that provides them with part of the sustenance they need and will not find at work; affection, understanding, sympathy, encouragement and a place to relax. These things are usually provided by their wives, and it is they who are many times the unsung heroes of success in small business. They should be, because when they send their man out in the morning, they must keep his home for him while he fights his way. His successes may make life easier for them, but it is the wives who also pay the price during the lean years.

So I dedicate this book to all the wives of all the small businessmen out of respect for their quiet courage and their sacrifices—and to my own dear wife Nan.

Foreword

Small business is an important, essential, integral part of our economic system. There are over four and one-half million small firms in this country representing 95 per cent of all American business concerns, and employing over one-half of all employed persons. In the manufacturing area, assuming "small" means a company with fewer than 100 employees, 94 per cent of all manufacturing companies are small; these employ 21 per cent of all manufacturing employees. If the definition is broadened to include companies with 500 employees, 99 per cent of all manufacturing companies are small and employ 40 per cent of all manufacturing employees.

In spite of dire predictions that it cannot compete in a world of giants, there is strong statistical evidence that small business is here to stay. Although hundreds of thousands of small firms disappear each year for one reason or another, other hundreds of thousands are formed to take their place; and the net result is an average increase of about 50,000 small firms per year in the United States. Several scholarly studies have come to the conclusion that although the situation varies somewhat from year to year, the relative position of small business in the American economy has remained fairly constant since about 1900, whether measured in percentage of total number of companies, assets employed, or total income.

Although we speak of "small business" as a collective noun,

Foreword

it should be remembered that the phrase covers infinite variety, a hodge-podge in a state of flux, including both the one-man fruit stand on the corner and the sophisticated manufacturer of high technology items for the space program. There is also wide variation, much more so than among large companies, as to profitability. At one end of the spectrum are numerous weak firms, poorly financed, poorly managed, and of doubtful viability. If, however, we examine the well managed, successful segment we find a quite different picture. We find companies that are not only participating fully in our dynamic economy but contributing to progress and a higher standard of living. Some are generating important parts of our continuing technological revolution; many are at the leading edge of technological advance. Small companies are well represented among firms with the highest growth rates and firms with the highest return on invested capital.

If we compare small company results with those of large companies we find that generally a higher percentage of small companies than of large ones are unprofitable. Approximately 85 per cent of failures are small companies. Of all companies showing losses the evidence indicates that the smaller the company, the greater the loss as a percentage of equity. On the other hand, of all companies showing a profit, the small companies show a higher return on investment than large ones. The least profitable small companies do worse than the least profitable large companies, and the most profitable small companies do better than the most profitable large ones. The profitability of small companies as a group fluctuates more than that of large companies between good times and bad, and shows a greater dispersion within the category as to profitability at any one time. The point of all this statistical analysis seems to be that in spite of the notoriously high infant mortality and well publicized financial difficulties of small firms, the well managed segment produces favorable and satisfactory results.

Foreword

These results suggest that there are attractive opportunities to invest in and manage small businesses. The figures also show that in spite of a very high turnover within the area, small business as a whole shows remarkable vitality and a persistent hold on its position in the economy. In my opinion, there are two important reasons for this healthy ability to endure. Small business fills essential economic needs, and also fills essential personal needs.

As to economic needs, it was mentioned earlier that several hundred thousand small businesses disappeared each year. Only a small percentage are actual failures. Mergers and acquisitions absorb many. A large number are sufficiently successful to outgrow the "small" category. There are many voluntary liquidations, for a variety of reasons. Many corporations serve a temporary purpose. Age, sickness, death, or just discouragement cause many proprietors to close up shop. Small retailers, wholesalers, manufacturers may find that a continually changing economy has reduced or eliminated their economic justification for continuing in business, even though the economy as a whole and their industry may be thriving.

While weakening or disappearing in some areas, small companies spring into life in others: motels, drive-in movies, slot machine laundries, franchise operations, service industries, and many types of manufacturing. For every new industrial development or scientific program (space, computers, nucleonics, electronics, etc.) small companies materialize to supply critical needs. As gaps or niches open up, disclosing unfilled needs, small business moves in. Sometimes the required volume is too small to interest a large company. Frequently the alertness, flexibility, or initiative of the small company enables it to move faster than large companies. It may have conceived of some bright innovation no one else thought of. Not infrequently a small, highly specialized company is able to meet specifications others cannot. Small companies are frequently not only fully competitive on the

Foreword

basis of quality, price, and service, but may have definite strategic competitive advantages. This may explain in part why, in spite of our famous giant and near-giant corporations, such a large part of our country's business is transacted by small companies, and why large companies rely so heavily on small companies on both the supply and sales side of the business. As the economy and large companies grow, there is a logical reason for the small company segment to develop proportionally.

Perhaps even more important than the supporting role played by small business is the creative one. Small business is to some extent the seed bed of the economy. New ideas, inventions, all sorts of innovations are conceived and introduced by small companies or result in the formation of new companies. These new companies serve as replacements for those that fade from the scene. They revitalize the economy, frequently by being acquired by an aging large company. Some of these small companies develop into the giants of the future.

Small business also fills an important and basic human need. People differ greatly in their "need to achieve," their risk tolerance, self-confidence, desire for independence, their frustration tolerance, and their impatience to break away from routine and do something challenging and exciting. Different people seek different outlets for their different drives. Space exploration, the Peace Corps, scientific frontiers attract certain groups. Small business has its own attraction and provides an outlet for the energy of the man with entrepreneurial drive, who craves to be on his own, and wants to make his own decisions and take the consequences. A business of his own also appeals to the man who wants an opportunity to build an estate more rapidly than he feels is possible working for someone else. For one who might have been a prospector for gold in another time, small business provides the opportunity to "strike it rich."

Others may prefer a small company career for reasons

Foreword

quite different from those just given. They may like especially the atmosphere and personal relationships. Some people are concerned with concepts and values related to individuality, variety, democracy, freedom, need for self-expression, moral satisfaction, sense of dignity, etc. The attraction of small business for some people seems to be based on the belief that these concepts are more attainable in small firms than in large. The infinite variety found in small business certainly gives a wide choice to those with individualistic tastes.

Since small business provides opportunities for both profit and personal satisfaction but shows wide dispersion around the average as to profitability and life expectancy, perhaps we should look at some of the typical problems. Although no statement will be uniformly true of all small companies, it is not unusual for both capital and management to be spread dangerously thin. Decisions are critical, with little margin for error, and are frequently made by one man, who may have inadequate background, inadequate assistance, and inadequate time for proper consideration. The product line may be highly specialized, with little diversification. Sales may be highly concentrated in very few markets; some small companies have just one customer. Risk may be very high, putting a premium on judgement, planning, versatility, resourcefulness, and prudence.

In various studies and surveys for the purpose of determining the causes of failure of small firms the principal problems seem to be deficiencies in capital and management. In my opinion if a company has good management, it is not likely to have financial problems. Apparently there is adequate capital for worthy projects, from banks, venture capital firms, small business investment companies and the Small Business Administration. I suspect that the most usual causes of chronic shortages are poor planning, recklessness, and a desire to maintain maximum equity control. This reasoning brings the spotlight to rest on management as the critical variable in small business success.

Foreword

Fortunately many people agree that the small business sector is important to our economy. Although there are numerous approaches to improving the chances for survival of small business, it seems to me that the most important assistance that can be given is in the management area. There are various ways of helping the small businessman to be a better businessman. The Small Business Administration has an active program of management assistance. Many large companies have training and educational programs for their small business customers, particularly dealers. Trade associations, especially those made up largely of small companies, are adding educational features to their programs, frequently in conjunction with a nearby educational institution. For example, the Smaller Business Association of New England has an annual three-day "live-in seminar" at the Harvard Business School. Other educational institutions, frequently with the cooperation of the SBA, conduct courses, seminars, and workshops for management people in local small companies.

In view of the importance of better management training needed to take full advantage of the opportunities in small business, it is surprising that more colleges and universities do not offer courses for the purpose. Here at Harvard Business School there has been for many years a lively interest on the part of the students in courses in small and new business, and in associated research report courses. There is also an active New Enterprise Club, and a Student Small Business Placement Program to seek out job opportunities in small companies that do not send recruiters to the School.

This important book by Louis Allen is a unique and useful addition to the educational material available in the area of small business management. It should be useful not only to managers who want to be better managers, but as encouragement to those thinking about striking out on their own. Louis Allen, the author, has been through the mill. He makes no bones about the difficulties but recommends that others

Foreword

try it. He has spent his business life managing, analyzing, and financing small business. He is a firm believer in small business as a satisfying and profitable career, and there is missionary zeal in his efforts to raise the level of small business management. This is shown by his much appreciated annual lectures to students at the Harvard Business School, his encouragement and financial support of research and education in the small business area, his efforts beyond the call of duty to be helpful to small companies in which his firm has invested, and of course by sharing the results of his experience and observations in the pages of this very useful book.

Frank L. Tucker
Professor
Harvard Business School

Introduction

Small business defies a definition that can be widely accepted. Mr. Allen directs his original and thoughtful comments to prospective new and established manufacturing businesses of moderate size. I will attempt to do the same.

In the early years of the teaching of business in this country, many of the courses revolved around institutions, such as the bank, the manufacturing company, the wholesaler and the department store. Later, the functional approach was introduced and such topics as production, selling, personnel, finance, and like subjects were developed. Today, more attention is being given to the individual, and the roles of the employer, the middle management man, the white and blue collar worker are discussed.

In small business, the key person is the owner. It has taken students of the subject, bankers, government men and even the owners of small business themselves a long time to come to this conclusion. Now, however, more of us are coming to realize that success in small business is based on the ability of the business owner or manager to make sound decisions.

This conclusion contradicts the long-held belief that money is the main ingredient in the success of small firms. This opinion was strongly held by the Congress of the United States when it wrote the legislation setting up the Small Business Administration, giving millions to its loan

Introduction

programs and tens of thousands to its management programs. This opinion is held by many bankers who scan the profit-and-loss statement and balance sheet of a small firm with care but often give minimum attention to the character of the management which is to return the loan with interest. Additionally, most owners of small businesses confidently believe that a loan will solve almost every problem they have, provided some private or public agency will make the loan at a reasonable rate.

Today, thinking on this subject is turning. If the management of a firm—or the promoters of a prospective business—have the capacity to make sound decisions in some depth and the ability to carry them out, financing can usually be found at a reasonable rate, even in times of tight money. The important and often relatively unknown element in such a proposal is management itself.

Educational institutions, through their teaching, their counseling and their research, are leading the way in this swing toward emphasizing the owner-manager as the key to success. The Small Business Administration is currently strengthening its management assistance in Washington and throughout the field. Bankers are giving more attention to the character and experience of new and older owners of business firms in considering loans. Businessmen themselves, especially those operating modest-sized establishments, are taking advantage of management training available to them while offering appropriate training to more and more of their own employees.

One factor which retards the improvement of management perception is the fact that many businessmen and some trainers fail to distinguish between business administration and business operation. Too many managers are so busy with day-to-day operations that they do not—so they say—have time to administer their business.

Profits, however, come from administration, and without sound administration, profits can be fleeting or non-existent.

Introduction

What is meant by administration? According to Koontz and O'Donnell (*Principles of Management*), they are Planning, Organization, Staffing, Direction, Control.

A large corporation can employ highly skilled people to head staff departments where these administrative functions are carried on, sometimes in great detail. In the small business, however, the owner often has to perform all these functions himself, while operating the business. One solution of this dilemma is to recognize the difference between administration and operation, to accept the importance and necessity of administration, and to set aside some time for administration.

Such action is particularly necessary for planning and controlling. A business without a plan is like a ship without a rudder. Before long, it will flounder and sink. Any business that is long without some controls will get out of hand. It may continue to operate but only at a loss and as long as its creditors permit.

BUSINESS GROWTH

Growth is a normal expectation for business as well as for people. With growth, comes greater service to the community, increased employment, and more substantial profits. Many firms, however, do not grow. Why?

There are probably many reasons, but here are a few:

(1) Lack of experience. It is not necessary to assume that in order to be successful in a particular kind of business the prospective businessman must have had long experience in managing that kind of business. In most instances, this would not be practical or possible. But the prospective operator certainly should know something as an employee about the administration and operation of the kind of business which he would like to start or buy. Businessmen have never found a sound substitute for experience.

(2) Lack of customer point of view. Even today, too many actual as well as prospective businessmen want to

Introduction

produce products which they have invented, which they need, or which they like. They give little or no attention to the broader needs of the public and its current desires, or to competition. In the buyers' market which is with us even today with tight money, the consumer makes the choice. The producer who has rightly anticipated the consumer's choice reaps the profits.

(3) Hesitation to hire others. Growth is handicapped sometimes by the inability of the owner to see the need of hiring a staff or line executive or his unwillingness to do so because of the additional cost involved. For example, he might see the wisdom of hiring another salesman but not a credit manager. He knows that he cannot do all the selling which has to be done but he may believe that he can handle credits, even though he is a trained engineer and creative product designer.

(4) Unwillingness to delegate authority with responsibility. Since many modest businesses start out as a one-man shop and since ownership and control belong exclusively to the originator of the firm, he often finds it difficult if not really impossible to delegate authority where it is needed to insure the growth of the business.

(5) Fear of the strange or new. Many busy operators shy away from the strange or new. Because they do not have time or take time to investigate, they ignore what may be some excellent policy, procedure, product, or employee. They operate to the exclusion of administration, and planning suffers.

(6) Fear of growth. Strange as it may seem, some new business owners are fearful of growth itself. They believe they are doing reasonably well with their present products and markets. They believe they and their staff, if they have one, are qualified to carry on a profitable business "as is." But if they try to grow, will they be equally successful? Maybe not. They are afraid to venture. They decide not to assume any additional risks. They are reasonably satisfied to remain just as they are.

Introduction

INGREDIENTS OF SUCCESS

The success of a business is measured in sales, employment, service to the community, and profits. The relative importance of each varies from case to case. Success, however, has to be earned. The question is, how do you earn it? Here are some factors that are involved:

(1) Experience. The promoter or owner of a business should have some experience in the same or a similar business as an employee. Inexperienced young people who want to open or buy a business of their own are often advised to first work for a time for a successful operator of the same kind of business and observe what makes him successful. Often such a businessman will take a personal interest in such an employee and later assist him to secure his own business when he is prepared to do so.

(2) Interest in people. Certainly, the owner or manager of any business, if he is to be successful, has to like people, like to be among them, enjoy group activities. He not only has to like people but be able to determine what these people—his potential customers—like and are ready to buy from him at the right price.

(3) Self-confidence. The foundation for success of any business is the owner's confidence in himself as owner, in the business which he has set up, in his policies, procedures, products, and services. A confident man will take the initiative, and a man with initiative will make decisions, the most important single action called for in business. If the confidence is based upon experience and knowledge, the results are apt to be profitable.

(4) Planning. The successful business has to be planned, just as the successful life has to be planned. It is hard to conceive that a businessman who does not plan can make many sound and profitable decisions over a period of time. The great value of planning is that it sets before the owner one or more goals toward which he can work. He may have to revise a goal now and then but he has something toward

Introduction

which to work, something which will help him to coordinate his production with his sales, sales with advertising, sales with credit extension, credit extension with money needs. Sound planning by the smallest business is imperative.

(5) *Delegation.* The growth and success of many firms has been the result of selecting employees able to assume responsibility and giving them the authority to carry out the duties assigned to them. Even if an employee makes a mistake now and then, his ability to make decisions within a prescribed area of management will increase his sense of responsibility and his value to the business. A "one-man" business can only grow up to the capacity of the manager and there it will stop until more administrative talent becomes available and is used by the owner.

(6) *Timing.* One quite important but often underemphasized ingredient of success in business is timing. An owner who through intuition or experience has a sense of timing is in a strong position to be successful. When should a particular product be placed on the market? When should it be redesigned? When should it be withdrawn entirely? These are important problems in any manufacturing organization and require constant study and reconsideration. With the increased tempo of business these days, the importance of good timing cannot be overemphasized.

(7) *Integrity.* To some persons integrity of mind and action may not seem important in a discussion of success these days. Today, big business tends to call in its legal counsel, place a proposed policy or procedure before him, and inquire whether such an action is legal. If the answer is "No," the idea is dropped. If the answer, however, is "Yes," usually the idea is adopted. The question of whether or not any moral implications are involved may be overlooked or ignored. However, the long-run success of large business as well as that of smaller firms is still measured in terms of the combined judgments of their potential customers, and customers are apt to favor the businesses which observe high moral principles and practices.

Introduction

(8) Flexibility. Today, with entire markets changing rapidly, with revolutionary methods appearing overnight, with the increasing use of computers and a developing technology, only a quite flexible management can long operate in the black. Flexibility of organization and personnel is a necessity today. This is an advantage which often accrues first to the smaller businesses in a competitive situation because of their ability to reverse themselves quickly if such action seems desirable. A large corporate body by necessity has to be more cautious and deliberate in making its decisions.

(9) Training. No longer is it desirable for a company to plan training programs inside or outside the business only for its blue- and white-collar workers and for middle management. Because of the rapidity of change, increasing competition in many industries and trades, and improved technology, the owner-managers themselves need training too. Business and vocational training for adults is growing at a rapid rate. For those who are ready for it, it can be found in many public and private sources.

The lot of the owner of a small manufacturing business is not an easy one. He has plenty of problems. As Mr. Allen says, he should look carefully and long into the question of becoming the owner of a small business. But if he feels he measures up to the requirements of such an assignment and is prepared to work harder than he has ever worked before, the rewards can be satisfying. Such an owner will find that he is meeting a need of his community, he is supplying products and services desired by his customers, he is giving fruitful employment to his workers, and in return for his services to his friends and neighbors, he is earning a net profit over and above a salary.

Dr. Wilford L. White, Director
Small Business Guidance and
   Development Center
Howard University
Washington, D. C.

Contents

Foreword   vii
Introduction   xv
Prologue   1

1. Three Characteristics of a Small Businessman   7
2. How to Raise Money for Your Small Business   21
3. How to Get Customers   53
4. How to Select Products   81
5. How to Manage Your Small Business   113
6. The Philosophy of a Venture Capitalist   141

Starting and Succeeding
In Your Own
Small Business

Prologue

I think everyone should undertake, at some time in his life, to create an enterprise in his own image. It need not be a vast, industrial organization; it might be something as small and parochial as a project for high school children. It need not even be an enterprise for profit. But every man should try his hand at it. The rewards are very much greater, the fruits of success much sweeter than the difficulties and problems to be met along the way.

In other words, "the price is right." The chance for overall gain is far greater than the risk of loss, and any businessman knows that when such a situation exists, he should act.

There is a qualification to my recommendation, however. An enterprise should be entered into properly, and for the correct reasons. As the reader will observe in the pages that follow, there are only a few reasons and only a few ways that I consider "right and proper." These are not definitive and I state them only imprecisely; although I wish very much that I could be both definitive and precise, I cannot, and there is the end of it.

Such is not the case with my reasons for writing this book, however. I definitely and precisely believe in small business. And the only way to keep small businesses coming along is to keep a good crop of small businessmen coming along.

When I was fourteen years old my parents sent me to

Prologue

Exeter, a prep school in New Hampshire. In those days before air shuttles and jets the journey from Cincinnati took all of 28 hours by train to Boston, a change of station, and again by train to New Hampshire. Because of the train schedules I had the choice of arriving either a day early or five hours late. My father decided I should arrive a day early.

I therefore arrived alone and made my way to the school, full of fear and apprehension. At the registration desk a huge man with white hair looked down at me and said, "Allen, you wretched thing, here is a book of rules, things you must not do. Read it." It was a thick book, or so it seemed to me. I picked it up and my heart sank at the thought of all those rules. "Mr. Curwen," I replied, "I would rather have a book on things I *can* do." D'Arcy Curwen, the man closest identified with Exeter and a legend in the accounts of preparatory schools in this country, looked at me for what seemed a long, long time. His reply was terse: "Read this, and learn it."

Six weeks later I was asked to leave the school.

Years later, when I was an undergraduate at Harvard, two of Mr. Curwen's sons were in my club and I had occasion to meet him. He told me that he had not forgotten my remark and had prepared a much smaller book of things one *could* do, but that it hadn't worked.

Despite the seeming ineffectiveness of the form, I decided to make this a book about the things a man *can* do in small business. There are some stories about failures but they point up what a man *did*, not so much to say that he was wrong, but to illustrate the fact that a man can do almost anything he chooses in small business. For him to be successful is another matter.

The best advice my father gave me concerning my career was when I was a freshman at college. He told me that I should seek out at least six men who had careers I admired. I should, if possible, interest them in my own career and keep them informed of my progress. He said I would find that such men would be pleased and complimented to be thus

Prologue

singled out and would be genuinely interested. He was right.

The finest businessman I have ever known is John P. McWilliams. He began his own company after some years of experience in his field. It grew and prospered and is today listed on the New York Stock Exchange. Others knew he was good, too. He was a Director of such companies as Union Carbide, Goodyear, Youngstown Sheet and Tube, Eaton Manufacturing, and National City Bank of Cleveland.

One time I had gone to Cleveland to see a bank about an important loan for the company I was working for. I called Mr. McWilliams and he asked me to spend the night at his house. During the evening I explained the nature of the loan I sought, its importance to the company, and related affairs. He said nothing.

In the morning, because it was snowing, he drove me to the Rapid Transit Line. As we pulled up he jumped out of the car and stopped a passing auto. Out of it stepped a tall, handsome man whom Mr. McWilliams introduced as the president of the bank. Mr. McWilliams put his arm around me and said, "I want you to meet Louis Allen. Take good care of him; he's one of my 'boys.'"

I then rode downtown with the president of the bank I was going to call on. I was so utterly unnerved by the recommendation that I did not ask for the loan because it seemed to me that Mr. McWilliams had more confidence in my program than I did, and I was not too sure of it myself. If anything had gone wrong, Mr. McWilliams would have been terribly embarassed, so I did not even ask or apply for the loan.

I remember this so well because it was a great lesson to me. Mr. McWilliams was right, of course; the loan would have been handled as well as the one I got at another bank. I was wrong because I lacked the confidence in my own judgment that comes from experience and knowledge. That is the great ingredient in success—confidence well placed and based on understanding.

Prologue

Another man I got to know in the same way is Mr. Wilfred Rice. I first met him nearly ten years ago in connection with the formation of a banking enterprise. Wil Rice must be one of the best bankers in America. He is not well-known outside of the New York metropolitan area because he is a man of complete modesty. But his record of lending and collecting, of building the bank of which he was vice-chairman when he retired is one of unparalleled success. He was my boss for five years.

The company was a Small Business Investment Company of New Jersey. We made financings of all kinds to small businesses. Wil Rice was the president, although his full-time job was as vice-chairman at a bank.

Wil Rice hired me one day when I had stopped by to see him on my way into New York City. The SBIC had only recently been formed and there was no active manager. I took a cut in pay of nearly 50 per cent and became a lender rather than a borrower. My early performance was terrible, but Wil is also a very great teacher and he was very patient with my shortcomings. Under his guidance he and I built a company whose profit record was second to none in this field, and whose record of service was the very highest. We were creative, imaginative, and tough. The years with Wil Rice were among the very best of my life.

This book is all about the things I have observed and thought about in my years as a small businessman. Throughout the book, I have written about events and situations in which I have been involved over all my years, and I have made no effort to pinpoint the time when, or the place where, they occurred in any but the most general way.

I have done this for the reason that I have mentioned and described these things since they illustrate an essential ingredient in business—that is the "feeling" one has for this or that. I took that job with Wil Rice because I had a "feeling" about it. That is the point I want to make. Every so often a situation comes along and one gets a reaction—a positive

Prologue

reaction—in his stomach. Trust these feelings; they are usually very reliable. An intuitive urge is an important ingredient in decision-making; it is the basis of what is called a man's "style." And whatever a man does he should develop his "style," his way of doing things.

I hope this book will encourage those men who have been thinking about going into business themselves to do it; and that those already so engaged will find in it justification for their actions.

I hope it will provide the small businessman with a basis for confidence in his own abilities, and that every person who reads this book will see something of the importance of developing a "feel" for his enterprise, whatever it may be—a "style," an intuitive sense that will shape his enterprise into his own image.

1

Three Characteristics of a Small Businessman

Several months after I had been hired by Wil Rice one of the company's directors asked him why he had hired me. "I know for a fact that Louis made every mistake in the book when he was in small business himself, but never the same one twice," he said. "Maybe he can spot the same mistakes in our client companies and check them before they get out of control." He then added, "But even with the mistakes he always seemed to run a profitable company."

As a recommendation, this seemed odd to me, but after thinking about it, I decided the best explanation was that it happened to be the truth, though I had never thought of it in just those terms. Then, just about that time I received a call from a professor at the Harvard Business School who was running the small business courses there. He asked if I could come on short notice to talk to his classes. There were two sections with over eighty students in each; the talk to each was to run one hour and ten minutes. Without hesitation I accepted, flattered beyond words, and eager to do it.

Then came the problem of topic. My friend had said he wanted the class to "see a real, live small businessman," so

Three Characteristics of a Small Businessman

that part was easy. But as to the subject matter, I was completely at sea.

It was necessary to arrange my calendar to be away that day, so in discussing a new date for a meeting already scheduled with my boss, I mentioned the reason for making the change. "What are you going to tell them, Louis?" he asked. I replied that I did not have the vaguest idea. "Why not tell them about your mistakes, then. You could certainly fill two hours with that—maybe even more."

There it was again, about the mistakes. However, these comments about mistakes were always delivered with a broad smile so, nothing loth, I did just that, and with good results, as it turned out, because my invitation has been renewed yearly since.

My mistakes have neither ruined me nor have they dampened my enthusiasm for small business. It might be said they are responsible for getting me into the investment business and providing me with the most pleasurable visits to my graduate school. In small business one has unlimited opportunity to be wrong as well as the same opportunity to be right, together with a good deal of power to act in most situations. This is probably the greatest pleasure I have had in my business career and it is the real spice in small business—the power to act and be right or be wrong.

The first "act" a small businessman takes is usually the basic decision to go out on his own. The decision may take months or even years to reach, or it may be a spur-of-the-moment affair. Sometimes it is forced on a man who must step into a family business. Whatever the process, whatever the circumstances, whatever the reasons, this first step is the most crucial decision a man is likely to make concerning his small business.

In effect, what has been made is the selection of a president or manager of a business. The man who begins a small business has *selected himself* to run the show, as it were. In almost every case I have seen (my own included, and I

Three Characteristics of a Small Businessman

believe in the vast majority of cases everywhere), the man who has done this selecting is neither qualified by training and inclination nor by objective reasoning to make such a judgment. This, more than any single ingredient in a small business, accounts for the high rate of failures and the marginal success characteristic of most small businesses.

When a man picks himself as "the boss" he has made a fateful choice—one on which the fortunes of his enterprise will rise or fall. So much depends on him from then on.

One of the very best descriptions of "the boss" I have ever heard came from a shop foreman. I was working in Cincinnati as a general roustabout in a manufacturing company and had been assigned a job involving the production of a variety of wooden parts for pianos. The shop foreman and I had discussed several plans and had narrowed the possibilities to two specific programs. We selected one and prepared what I thought to be a persuasive and compelling case, thoroughly documented and complete.

Before undertaking the program, the president of the company, Paul Rodgers, came down to see the results. He looked at our proposal with interest, thought about it for a few minutes and then told us we were wrong, that our program would create problems and he gave us his suggested way of handling the entire matter. I was utterly undone.

Three months after that, when it was obvious Mr. Rodgers was entirely correct, I asked the foreman how he supposed Mr. Rodgers had known what should be done. His answer will always remind me of the undefinable sixth sense of what is proper, essential to the leader of a business: "Because he's the boss, and that's why he is, and we ain't."

No book about personnel management, to my knowledge, devotes any significant amount of space to the selection of people for small business ownership. Unlike the giant firm which has recruiting and selection experts to screen the wheat from the chaff, the small business firm, which comprises the most common economic unit in our business sys-

Three Characteristics of a Small Businessman

tems, cannot afford to employ a personnel manager. The end result is that in the 4.5 million businesses in this country, the vast majority of which are small, the top managers have been through a rather unsystematic personnel selection process in terms of conventional personnel theory. More than that, there's something very special about the selection of the owners. Let me say it again: *They have selected themselves.*

Study a dozen texts in employment and selection, and you'll find none has a chapter or even a paragraph to cover the problem of the man who must screen himself for top management in his own small firm. I maintain this is generally the most misunderstood and underrated area of small business—that is, the importance of proper selection of "the boss."

When I first was asked to speak on small businesses, it seemed advisable to get some sort of reading of the ideas held by the class about small business. To get such a reading, I presented the students with the following situation:

Assume you are thinking of purchasing control of a manufacturing concern. Your analysis is thorough and you can state absolutely the facts of the company's condition. In descending order of importance, rank the following results of your investigation:

1. The plant and equipment are old and need attention.

2. After deducting the purchase price, you have left what you consider to be barely adequate funds to supplement working capital.

3. The existing management you will inherit is old in age but has many years' experience in this field.

4. You, personally, have less than three years' actual working experience in this industry.

5. The company's product or products meet the needs of a broad class of customers, and well-established distribution methods exist in this industry.

Based on these assumptions, would you go ahead or not?

Three Characteristics of a Small Businessman

If your answer is "yes" or "no," list the facts for or against your decision.

I have tested this short questionnaire with a sample sufficiently large to justify the statement that most people make their first and cardinal mistake when they decide to enter a business venture on their own. Of my sample of nearly 750, including Harvard Business School students and two other groups, 18 people have ranked question number 4 as their first decision point. That is a little better than 2 per cent, a percentage surprisingly close to the national average for success after ten years for small businesses.

This in no way surprises me. I have made the same mistake myself, and of the many men I have known who went into business for themselves, most of them did so for all the wrong reasons. It is natural to be subjective about this kind of decision and there is no formula I know of that can be used to assist the man who wants to go into his own business. It is also my view that it would be impossible to catalogue or prepare a list of do's and don'ts. Every man who is just starting his own business, or just thinking about it or who may already be in business for himself has a background probably different from any other man; thus, the impossibility of any set type of analysis.

There is one ingredient, however, which I have observed to be very much a part of the small businessmen who succeed and very lacking in those who fail: *a willingness to "pay the price."*

About three years ago, in the course of one day, I had appointments with two different groups. One group consisted of three engineers from a national electronics firm who wanted to start a business of their own. The other group consisted of an engineer with an electro-mechanical background and a CPA who wanted to start their small business. The story of what happened to these two groups illustrates the point I want to make, i.e., a small businessman's success

Three Characteristics of a Small Businessman

will be measured in direct proportion to the sacrifices he will be willing to make in order that his small business succeed.

The three engineers sat across my table and outlined their background. Each was making over $25,000 a year, was married and had several children. Their program was to start a business of their own in a line of products directly related to the work they were doing for their present employer. Their program was beautifully presented in an impressive binding with five-year forecasts and a complete analysis of all the salient facts. Naturally, I was quite impressed. They needed $350,000, and when I asked the question, "How much can you come up with as a group?" the spokesman for them said, "Just a minimal amount, perhaps $25,000." I next asked them what salaries they were willing to work for and explained that it was certainly no crime in this day and age to be poor. I also said I was not impressed with the savings that they were able to accumulate, so I naturally assumed all they had to put into this business was their time, and thus I was interested in the charges they would levy for their efforts. After a brief consultation between them, the consensus was that they might be able to reduce their salaries to $20,000 apiece. At that point, it was completely obvious they had no idea what self-selection into a small business meant, and they were completely unprepared for what lay ahead, in spite of the fact that their brochure was one of the most complete that I have ever seen.

The other group that I talked to that day consisted of just two men, the engineer and the accountant. Like the first group, they started off by telling me that the engineer was now making $18,000 a year and that the CPA had a practice which he and his wife ran in which they had gross draw of $15,000 after expenses. Their first statement was that they had, jointly, been able to save $15,000 and that this amount was completely committed to the program. Furthermore, the engineer went into some detail with me to show how it would be possible to keep his family together and meet

Three Characteristics of a Small Businessman

minimum expenses on $8,500 a year, a reduction in pay of $9,500 from the $18,000 he was currently earning.

Also, the CPA stated flatly that he was willing to give up two days a week of his own time and a day a week of his wife's time to work directly for the company at no charge. They then presented me with a program of projected sales and income which was broken down in such a way that the investment could be made step by step with a review at each period. This program showed an ultimate need of $200,000 from the investor. The profit potential as outlined by the second group was roughly similar to that of the first, although the product line was technically different.

I recommended to my loan committee that we make an investment in the second group and, of course, give a complete turn-down to the three engineers in the first group. Four and a half years later the situation was this: The first group of engineers had found investors to put up the $350,000, and when that turned out to be insufficient got another $150,000 from the same investors. The company that they formed is bankrupt, and all of the invested capital has been lost. Ostensibly, it was salary costs that ate them up. Actually, they had selected people (themselves) who wouldn't pay a present price for future success.

The second group now has a sales volume running at an average of $60,000 a month, and their profit is just a little better than 27 per cent on sales before depreciation and taxes. The president of the second group is now drawing $18,000 a year salary, and the accountant, although he is no longer associated with the company because of a new situation that presented itself, has been paid a fair price for the original cash investment which he made. It is the contention of the writer that given a half-decent idea for a needed product or service, the first essential in a small business is selection of the man or men who will run the business. I have never seen a small businessman go broke if he was willing to make the necessary sacrifices. On the other hand,

Three Characteristics of a Small Businessman

nearly every small business failure which I have seen is a direct result of a lack of willingness to make the appropriate sacrifices on the part of one or more of the principals.

A few well-known ideas: "Bread cast upon the waters," or perhaps, "Ask not what your business can do for you, etc. . . ." apply in the early years and formative periods. This does not mean to say that great personal sacrifices always accompany the successful growth of a small business, because sometimes good fortune and other events work towards the situation in which the progress is made without the attending sacrifices. Nor will self-sacrifice make up for a hopeless product or service nobody wants.

I would like to touch just briefly on several of the other important areas of personal sacrifices which seem to me fundamental in terms of the commitment that a man must make before he goes out on his own, or that he should make now if he is already running his own show.

One area requiring major sacrifice is well-documented by a conversation I had a short while ago. A gentleman who was very highly recommended came into my office. In his opening remarks he said the following, "I like the idea of forming my own sales representative organization." There are two things that are basically wrong with this statement, and they are among *the most common mistakes* I have observed on the part of self-selected small businessmen. The first thing wrong with the statement is that a man, and particularly a small businessman, cannot afford the luxury of indulging himself in an avocation that he "likes." If you pick yourself for top man in your firm because you think in so doing you'll avoid the menial or unpleasant jobs, your selection is weak. The world is full of very capable individuals who are doing an excellent job at their assigned tasks. Therefore, my first comment to this young man was that he spend some time learning what he must do to make his business succeed and then force himself to learn to like it. Hopefully, he might prove most competent as a salesman, but the proof

Three Characteristics of a Small Businessman

was needed. He wanted to select himself as head of his own sales organization because he disliked his present job.

The second thing wrong with his opening remark is somewhat similar. No one who has taken the trouble to look into the problems and the attendant sacrifices which have to be made by small businessmen could possibly say that "he would like to be a small businessman," that is, unless he is a glutton for punishment. The reason why a man selects himself to head his own small business is because he *must* do it. The American dream is made up of such urges. The drives which force him to do this are as old as capitalism itself. A man may have complete security as somebody else's employee, where he is fed, clothed, housed, where his medical needs are taken care of, but where he has fewer prerogatives of his own. On the other hand, the individual who wishes to accept the responsibility for providing his own security has complete freedom of choice in selecting the means for providing the security he wishes. Thus, in return for abdicating his individual prerogatives, one individual may choose the security which some, rather facetiously, have compared to being in jail, while the other individual may choose to be hungry or cold or sick or any combination of these conditions merely for the privilege of determining his own future. Thinking that "owning my own business is all rosy" is an illusion.

No doubt there are other considerations which are important; but nothing overrides the essential fact that starting and operating a small business is at once exhausting, exasperating, sometimes discouraging, always long hard work. It is also the most unbelievably satisfying work a man can undertake. That is why there are so many small businesses in our country.

Some day I hope to run across a situation where a man who wants to start a small business, or is already engaged in one, will hire a better man than himself to run it. That will be the millennium. I have never seen it in small business, al-

Three Characteristics of a Small Businessman

though there are several examples of much the same thing in larger business. General Electric paid an exorbitant price (or so it seemed) to acquire a small company just to get Steinmetz, and Mr. Edwin Land, the founder of Polaroid Company, hired the best man he could find to be president of his company while he took the position of Director of Research.

There is, of course, the problem of reasoning. If a man is truly interested in building a business he will "pay the price" by getting the best man available to run it—even if that man is not himself. This takes a dedicated and ruthless approach to the problem. Most men who start their own business have as a paramount thought the idea that they will "be their own boss," a half-truth at best. But they work on this thought until it becomes an obsession with them.

The engineers I mentioned earlier did not say it to me, but in the recent past I had occasion to meet some men with whom they had been associated. What I had assumed was confirmed; those engineers wanted to be free of working for someone else. They wanted to be their own bosses, run their own show. They would very likely have been discharged had they not left on their own. While their objectives were admirable, they were either unwilling, or unaware of the necessity, to spend the time to learn all about their proposed operation, to start in a small way and grow from a modest beginning. They wanted to burst full-grown on the electronics scene and they wanted to be free of any of the encumbrances of working for a large concern. Their doom was foretold by the conditions of their beginning.

There are many tragic histories written by men who went into business for the wrong reasons or on the wrong basis. One such man comes immediately to mind. He was one of the first prospects who came into my office for financing. He was in the millwork and woodworking business, and was doing a considerable volume and seemed to be making a profit, yet he was continually pressed for cash. The situation

Three Characteristics of a Small Businessman

was sufficiently interesting to warrant a visit to his plant, which I made very shortly thereafter. Having once been in the sawmill and logging business myself, I can state without fear of contradiction that this man had the most beautifully equipped shop I had ever seen. I admired his plant immensely. Here was his problem: He could not control himself in the acquisition of machinery. This man eventually ended up in bankruptcy, and his machinery account, which had a book value of over $600,000, was sold at auction for $92,000.

This man had a fixation for machinery. Later it transpired that his previous employer had thought of discharging the man because of his addiction to machinery. I think it is safe to assume this man had gone into business for himself so that he could exercise his insatiable appetite for machinery—certainly a reason not conducive to a successful enterprise.

Another time a man I had known for several years stopped in to see me and said that he desperately needed some financing for his business. Upon examination he indeed appeared to have a cash problem. The facts showed that he had been drawing some $3,500 a month salary out of his business because that was the amount he required to continue the living standard which he and his wife had adopted while he had been employed by a very large national concern in a top executive post. My friend had left this business in order to go into business for himself, and he had done quite well at the start. Was this a cash problem? On the surface it seemed so, but it was more than money.

I was much distressed to have to tell my friend that before I could help him, he would have to reduce his salary to not more than $1,500 a month. This was a very unacceptable proposition to him, and he left in somewhat of a huff. Several weeks later, he came back saying that he had found that other bankers with whom he had talked had adopted an attitude like mine, and since he was going to have to cut back on his living standards, he would prefer to do it with an old friend rather than with a stranger, and would I still do it?

Three Characteristics of a Small Businessman

The answer was "yes." My friend then did the following things. He sold his house, which was a beautiful place, and moved into a small modest home which he rented. He put the proceeds of the sale into his business. He let his maid go. And in other ways he reduced his requirements so he could keep his family going on the $1,500 a month. Very happily his business continued to prosper and, with the adequate cash produced by a new self-perception, the future of his business looks very bright indeed. Was it the cash alone that tipped the scale? Hardly. It was the eased pressure and his determination to place his long-run goals ahead of immediate income.

So much for some case histories. What does it take to make this first decision and make it right? I have prepared a check list which I use when a new prospect comes to see me about financing his business.

1) *Does the man comprehend the gravity of his actions?* The few examples I have given show only isolated instances of men who did not adequately comprehend what they were doing. I have sometimes thought that, next to getting married, the most awesome decision a man makes is to go into business for himself. Doing it for the wrong reasons will end in the equivalent of divorce, a situation just as unpleasant and heartbreaking.

2) *If the man is fully aware of his actions, is he sufficiently motivated to stick it out?* Progress is almost always erratic in small business. Sometimes the first run of success is followed by failures and slow times. Most often progress is slow from the start, and discouragement is the order of the day. Self-discipline is absolutely essential at this point. In order to pass this point a man must convince me he is willing to make every possible adjustment in his personal life as may be dictated by the affairs of the business. As a friend of mine once said of this attribute, "You can't be a little bit pregnant." He was right. The question is total commitment, total dedication.

Three Characteristics of a Small Businessman

3) *Does the man know his business?* The mere fact of desire, motivation, call it what you will, is still not sufficient to score 100 per cent in this check list. A man should know what he is about, and the only way he can learn this is by doing. This takes many years, usually. Experience in a similar business is the best possible training. But sometimes it isn't possible for the man to get this training. In that case, and providing his experience has been comparable and successful, the man can still pass muster with me if he scores high on Items 1 and 2. A good man can learn about his particular business if given time. Proper motivation and a full comprehension of what he is doing will usually buy him the time he will need.

It's just about that simple. As with most things, there is nothing mysterious or unclear; these are the same qualities that will get a man to his objectives in most situations.

In small business the errors a man makes are noticed sooner, cost him more and hamper his future on a greatly aggravated scale compared with similar situations in large enterprises. The biggest disadvantage of being small is the inability to absorb error. Thus, a proper beginning is essential if error is to be avoided in the formative stages, just as it is essential for later errors to be corrected and eliminated in the future.

2

How to Raise Money for Your Small Business

A few years ago one of the state universities' extension schools asked me to speak at a meeting of small businessmen. I had understood that my subject was to be the marketing aspects of small business. This was a dinner meeting, one of a series of meetings held at supper time, to which some fifty small businessmen had subscribed. My host and I were talking with the other men at the supper table when one of them said, "I'm glad that you're going to talk about how to get money for your small business because that's a big problem with me." It was a big problem with me, too, because I had not prepared remarks on that subject and I looked at the course director with some puzzlement. He was just as puzzled, and the matter was resolved by looking at the program which had been printed for the students. The course director had laid out the subjects for the various evenings and had assumed, improperly, that the administrative department had followed his format. But in some way, known best to the administrative personnel, the dates on the program had been altered. There was nothing to do but to talk on the subject of finance.

How to Raise Money for Your Small Business

Without having very much more preparation than that, I duly took the rostrum. Half facetiously I made the opening statement that the only way I knew to get a bank loan was to prove to the banker that you didn't need the money, and further stated that this axiom was proved by the well-known fact that banks would always lend money to a rich man or to a man of modest means who happens to have government bonds to put up for his collateral.

It was one of the best talks I ever gave, and I have since come to the conclusion that, taken with a grain of salt, what I said really is the best way to get a bank loan, and I offer it here as such.

A bank is interested in:
1) How much money you need.
2) How you are going to use it.
3) Whether your business will make more money.
4) Whether the bank will be repaid.
5) And when that will be.

But I believe that this is still not enough. The banker must also believe that the applicant can get along without the money, and my talk that night was pointed to the ways that a man can prove to a bank that he doesn't need the loan for which he is applying. And believe me when I say that *no small business ever failed because of a lack of funds*. The supply of funds and the availability of cash to meet your company's obligations is merely a thermometer that measures the wisdom and discipline with which you have committed your funds. When and if you run clean out of working cash, your thermometer reading is zero. It indicates your inability to live within your means.

When you are applying for a loan or when you are seeking investors, do *not* use the time-worn phrase, "with a little more cash I could really go places," or words to that effect. If the man you are talking to knows anything about small business he will spot you for a fool who doesn't know much about running a company. He will assume, as he must assume, that his funds will go down the same rat hole as the other money, and you won't get your financing.

In the first chapter I told about two different groups of people who had seen me in the course of one day; the three engineers and the man and his accountant. One of the strongest points in my recommendation to finance the proposition presented by the second group was the fact that they could actually have gotten along without any extra money. Their progress would have been slow and their personal sacrifices would have been great, but they were already making those sacrifices and were already living within their means. Although their proposal was much less precise than the engineers' and did not come in a fancy brochure, their story was believable because they could demonstrate that they did not have to have the money to continue.

With the three engineers it was entirely different. They could not even get started without the money, and a large part of the funds they required was going to go to support their high wage requirements. This is obviously very uninteresting to a banker. How these three men succeeded in convincing an institution to put up the money for their venture remains a mystery to me. But the results were inevitable. The losses incurred by all the creditors as a result of the business formed by the three engineers were in excess of three-quarters of a million dollars.

In preparing a proposal to get some financing for your business a successful format is the one I mentioned earlier. First, *how much money do you need?*

You probably won't believe this, but 50 per cent of the loan applications I see ask for more money than is required. For some reason small businessmen in particular have a great tendency to overstate their cash requirements. This probably stems from the chronic pressure they are under for cash, a condition that very likely leads them to conclude that a lot of cash would provide a means of escaping the bothersome insistance on payment by their creditors.

How to Raise Money for Your Small Business

They overstate their requirements because they usually want enough cash to clean up every debt that is hanging over them. In America we have developed the concept of amalgamating our bills into one bank or finance company loan with "one easy payment," a procedure that may work well for one individual but doesn't work in a small business.

There is a cardinal rule, particularly in small business: *Everybody that's already in, stays in.* By this I mean that the money that has already been put in the business usually will have to stay in and usually will be subordinate to the new money. If small businessmen will remember this, they will have learned an important point that can make the difference between getting their money or getting turned down.

Whenever money is loaned to a small business, the business from then on has a creditor who will want to get paid. If the terms of the loan are such that the creditor can insist on payment or make life so miserable for the company that any new potential lender becomes discouraged, that loan may be the last loan the small business will get.

Someone once said that "when good becomes hungry, it will seek food even in dark corners." Many a small businessman has made the mistake of putting himself in bad hands, delivering himself and his business to the sharks. This is done because of the pressure under which the small businessman sometimes operates—pressure brought about by a shortage of cash.

I remember a case where a good little company got a loan from a local businessmen's group because one of the group happened to be a friend of the small business operator. It was a secured term loan that provided the operator with the cash he then required, plus much more extra cash than he should have been given. All went well and the business grew as the operator undertook to employ his extra cash. Quite naturally, after a while this growth created cash needs over and above the funds he had been given. He went back to the businessmen's group and told his story. In the interim, this group had had three other loans go bad on them and had decided they would abandon their financing efforts. Therefore, they told the operator they had no more funds to advance him.

In the following month, the operator spent most of his time running from one bank to another, at first leisurely, then frantically, seeking additional money. It was at this point he came to see me. By now his business was suffering from his absence and his other creditors were giving him trouble. The amount of funds he now needed was enormous for his size of operation because he had let the interest slip on his term loan in order to meet his payroll, and the businessmen's group had declared a default. They declared the entire loan due and payable, and the operator now needed enough to pay them off in addition to fresh cash for growth.

I spoke with the group's representative. He was adamant. They would not stay in under any basis. Within another six weeks the operator saw his business fail and the sheriff sell his assets off to satisfy creditors. The work of ten years and all his savings were lost.

What was his mistake? It was very simply that he had gotten more cash than he needed; and he had gotten it under terms that made further financing impossible without the lender's consent, and he had gotten it from an organization that was not professional. He did not really know how much money he needed, so he had followed the philosophy of old Sam Gompers. When asked what he was going to seek in the way of a labor contract, that venerable gentleman always replied "more," a condition good for labor, but not a basis for projecting financial needs.

I want to make the flat and definite statement again that a lack of cash was *never* the reason a small business failed. Yet, almost without exception, small businessmen who have lost their businesses will cry, "If only I had had another $10,000, I could have made it." Believe me when I tell you that a shortage of cash is only symptomatic of excesses in other areas of a business. There again is the problem of discipline and control. Bankers like to feel that from a perusal of a company's financial statement they can pinpoint these excesses. Once they have done this they know a great deal about the operator of the business.

Take the cases of the two men I spoke of earlier. The man who had the fixation about owning machinery presented a financial statement that reeked of this excess. No conceivable amount of cash would satisfy his desire for more equipment. Any new funds would thus be applied either to pay off past acquisitions or to pay for new and more outrageous purchases.

The other man had drawn too much salary. This was an excess easily overcome once the man made up his mind to exercise some discipline.

Let me remind all small businessmen—practicing or potential—that *discipline is a prerequisite to success.* If the small businessman's first act is to select himself as the president or leader of an organization, his second act may well be the raising of the required funds, or, if he has started with his own funds, the application for further funds for expansion. Whatever the situation, the potential investor will look at *how much* is being proposed. And he will note any areas that seem to indicate an excess of one kind or another. If he finds one, the application will probably be declined.

How does one avoid an excess? It is a question of *balance.* Every now and then, unhappily only too infrequently, I will have an application presented to me which shows the "balance" a good operator builds into his business. This man presents a picture of cash needs growing out of a balanced operation. He may need cash to finance larger sales and the inventories required—but he has not already taken on those sales. He has arrived at the point where additional sales can be made, but he has stopped short of taking them while he is getting his financing. How much more attractive this type of investment is than one where the trouble has already started because the operator is looking for his money after he has taken on the sales. Or, the man may need more machinery to undertake production of orders. Again, the same thing will apply.

When a man who seeks money can show that he has *disciplined* himself—has controlled his operation to reach a point where he can swing his cash needs and has then *stopped* until he can obtain additional cash—he has shown by his actions that he is not only a good operator in the sense of living within his means, but also that he knows how to *use* money.

It is a near universal observation that all but a very few small businessmen have even an understanding what money is, let alone an ability to manage it properly. Cash is a commodity in the same sense that fertilizer is a commodity: when applied to a field it produces an improved crop. Cash is an "agent for growing something." It is the oil that lubricates a machine. If this oil is not applied regularly the machine will not operate properly and it will wear out before its time; just as fertilizer when applied irregularly will produce irregular crops. Too much fertilizer at once is just as bad in its own way as none at all. Every now and then I go all out on my lawn at home and really put down that good chemical fertilizer. The results are always the same—big brown spots of burnt up grass.

The same is true of a business; the application of too much of the commodity called cash has the same effect. Our economists say of the national economy that it is "overheated." They mean the lawn is going to burn itself out with too much growth.

So when you are applying for that all-important loan, and your application is being reviewed, be sure you can show the first essential—*a need that has developed from a "balanced" operation*, one without excesses. You will also have avoided the problem of forcing someone out who's been in.

That is another point to remember when you are financing

How to Raise Money for Your Small Business

your business: Don't get anybody "in" you may later have to get "out." This means that you should apply only to the biggest and best banks or other financial institutions. They are professionals who are in a specialized business. They are in business to stay and they won't loose their "cool" if things get tough. There never was a banker yet who expected a cash projection based on forecasted operations to come out the way it was planned. He expects things to change, to be different. He also expects to be kept informed of the changes from the forecast. More on that later.

There are many ways to plan the cash a small business will need. I have always found that a potential lender or investor is more interested in a proposal when the application is a forecast of operations at several levels. This provides the basis for a good discussion on the pros and cons of running the small business at various volumes or under different circumstances. It brings the lender or investor into the planning stage and allows him to work out, with the small businessman, a program which makes sense.

For example, one application I reviewed recently was submitted by a man who was operating a dry-cleaning establishment. He had done quite well and the business had provided his family with a good income *after* he had set enough aside to run the business. His proposal was for funds to acquire another establishment serving an adjoining community. He also needed funds for new trucks and some additional equipment.

The establishment he was purchasing had its own equipment at one location, but he proposed to expand his equipment at one location and do all processing in his present store. The newly acquired store would be only a pick-up and delivery operation.

But the total amount required under this plan was large in relation to his present net worth, so he had made another forecast under which the new store would be maintained with its own processing operation for the present, with the consolidation to come later. On this more modest program he also provided an estimate of the amount needed to have the existing trucks repaired and repainted as compared with purchasing new units.

I was very receptive to his second program and assisted him in putting it into good order. We declined to finance this man because the investment did not fit our own pattern at the time. However, I introduced him to several other groups where he found just the people to give him what he required.

This application was successful because, for one thing, it showed about how much money would be needed for several programs, and provided for a feasible program the planning of which involved the investor and the operator working *together*.

So you have been able to show your need for funds on a basis that is entirely acceptable. Next comes the question *how you are going to use it?*

Here, again, there are certain very important benchmarks. I can think off-hand of a half-dozen cases in which an application failed on this point when everything else was okay. In each of these cases there was a similar pattern: The operators wanted to branch out into something unrelated to what they had been doing.

One of the cases involved a company that was in the meat-processing business. It was just at the time when lots of small electronics companies were starting up and financing was very easy. This operator wanted to go into the electronics business to "diversify" his meat-processing operation.

This was an old, well-established operation which had a history of 20 years of profits. The financial statement was lovely, showing a liquid condition and no debt of a long-term nature. What I could not figure out was why the operator thought this qualified him to get into electronics. The reader can guess what happened after he obtained his financing elsewhere and got into the specialized area of solid state electronics.

Usually, when a small businessman comes in for financing he shows the funds as going to pay off some other pressing debts. This violates the rule of thumb, "everybody that's in, stays in." It is very uninteresting to a banker to contemplate the existing creditors congratulating themselves on getting paid off with the banker's money.

This is not to say there are not many appropriate circumstances where new funds can go to repay existing debt. In these cases the debt is actually cast into another form or over a longer time span. The potential lender does not consider his money as going to "pay" existing debt; he understands his money will pay off an existing obligation and accepts this fact because he also understands that the existing debt, not by its amount but by its terms, is causing the trouble.

That is to say, the new money he is putting up is really for the purpose of *changing* the debt structure of the business so as to provide, for example, a moratorium on principal payments, or the recasting of accounts payable (a current liability) into long-term debt. The latter case might be appropriate because it would provide the company with the ability to take discounts on its purchases after having cleaned up its existing bills with a given supplier.

Recently I put together some financing which illustrates these points. Two men who had been employed by a small business had purchased the company from the large, national concern of which it was the wholly owned subsidiary. They had effected the transaction by putting $1/10$ of the purchase price up in cash, and the national concern parent company had taken back a purchase money mortgage on the balance. This note was to be paid in equal quarterly installments, with interest, over five years. It was secured by what amounted to all the assets of the business.

The two men took charge. In the first year their accomplishments were fantastic. Sales tripled. One-third of the new business was attributable to the increase in the market for their company's products and about two-thirds was business they got away from their competitors. They also increased the gross profit on all sales by reducing costs and increasing prices. Also, their general and administrative expenses went down because they reduced their own salaries and did not have the extra burden of "home office" expenses.

There was a problem, however. The increased sales were putting an increased operating cash requirement on the business somewhat in excess of the operation's cash throw-off. The principal payments to the former parent company were heavy and required cash, and since the company was a new one with no loss carry forward or after-tax shelter, there was Uncle Sam looking to get his share of the profits. It all added up to an increasing cash bind.

The company had been partially covering this bind by arranging liberal terms with its suppliers. But the two operators came to the conclusion that this was only a temporary measure at best. (In this they were entirely correct. Suppliers want to be helpful, but they are not really in the financing business and should be used for that purpose only as a stop-gap.)

When the situation had been explained to me we worked out a program where the funds advanced were used to pay off the former parent concern and to pay off all the past due accounts payable. This amount was advanced on a ten-year basis with no payments on principal for three years. Then, in order to provide the company with some fresh cash, a bank loan was arranged with which the company could take the available discounts on its purchased supplies and materials. The discounts were sufficient to pay the interest on all of the bank loan and one-quarter of long-term advances!

This financing went almost entirely to recast existing debt obligations. In this case there was no loss in paying off existing debt because here the situation was actually one of giving the company some "breathing room."

How to Raise Money for Your Small Business

Another case was the opposite situation. A company in a new and expanding industry had gotten off to a good start. Within two years it was making good profits and had been able to show some profits in every quarter since its inception. Then it branched out into what seemed a logical extension of its existing business. The losses in this new venture were very heavy and almost equalled the profits of the original product lines. For two more years the company struggled with this new venture and finally abandoned it.

But during these same two years, its original lines had met expanded market acceptance and there was a heavy cash requirement developing there. Coupled with the tremendous drain created by the losses on the new venture, the cash requirements had forced the company to take on considerable financing. The operators had done this on a patchwork basis with little dribs and drabs of funds from one source or another.

After they had explained this situation to me, they presented their financing proposal. It showed that a very large percentage of the required funds would go to re-cast the debt created by the new venture. The remainder would finance the original business only partially since the total amount required to re-finance the combined debt attributable to the original lines and the abandoned newer lines was more debt than the company could support. This meant that any re-financing would be incomplete at best.

We declined the offer on the basis that even with the good profits from the original lines the company could not service the debt hanging over from the newer lines. There was much disappointment in our report to the operators of this business but we went to great lengths to point out our reasons. The memo we wrote developed the same point I want to make here. The bulk of the funds would pay off creditors whose advances had gone to support a loss operation. If they stayed in and agreed to terms over a long period, we would re-finance the always profitable and expanding original lines.

How to Raise Money for Your Small Business

The creditors whose funds had supported the loss lines would not agree to this. They were also in a position to exercise great pressure and control over the remaining business. In this case, because the original lines were demonstrably attractive, the company was sold to a large national concern. Had there been no such attractive feature the company would have surely failed.

These examples have shown only a few of the situations of proper or improper answers to the question: *How will the money be used?* There are as many examples of the improper answers as there are mistakes made by small businessmen. The proper and acceptable answers are similar to the case I described earlier. The funds should be for a constructive purpose, not to bail someone out.

Every now and then, however, people who are in will agree to stay in a bad situation. This almost always is limited to those times when there is an unacceptable loss to the creditor if the business fails and where he also cannot control the situation sufficiently to demand payment as his price for not forcing the business to liquidate. Such instances are rare in small businesses because the amounts of money involved are usually small taken in comparison with the amounts of debt given to larger companies. Therefore, most frequently in a small business the creditor can accept a loss because it is not "large" in his terms.

In small business, particularly, the operator will almost always have to pay off his creditors. That is why he should pick them so carefully for stability, terms, size, understanding and especially experience in small business.

Having, hopefully, shown how much you need and what it is going for, the next step is to demonstrate *how the new money will improve profits.*

This may be the hardest part of the presentation because here your success will depend on your ability to convince a man trained to be skeptical that something good will happen in the future. Believe me when I tell you that the best proof of the future is the past, and if you have a history as an unprofitable operator your problem is going to be very large indeed.

One time when I was young and working for a small business in the midwest I had gone to Washington to see the Small Business Administration. They are an agency of the government created to handle the entire complex of problems relating to small business in this country. My appointment was for the afternoon, so I spent the morning walking around. Outside the National Archives Building I was standing next to a family group who were also from the midwest. The youngest boy, who was probably eight or nine, looked at the building and read aloud the inscription on the façade: "What is past is prologue." He asked his father what that meant. The father replied, "Boy, that means you ain't seen nothing yet." I have always remembered that as the best of all possible translations of a great phrase into the American idiom. It is true when you ask a banker for money. All of us look at the past as the "prologue" of the future. If yours has been a *well-disciplined* and *balanced* operation it need not have shown tremendous profits; it probably hasn't. Living within your means and avoiding excesses is hard precisely because it causes things to come slower. But you had better understand that it is essential.

Eight out of every ten small business operators who come to my attention have not been able to work in this fashion. Two years ago I started to keep a tally sheet of these cases which I could later follow up. Of course there were instances where I was wrong, where a man who had done everything wrong somehow changed and got on the right track. Mostly, however, the poor operators stayed poor operators.

When you present a proposition to your prospective investor and you can show that your operation has been even marginally profitable, your projections are probably going to be believed. Sometimes your projection of profits may be believable even though your operation has been losing

How to Raise Money for Your Small Business

money. I always try to look beyond what the man is telling me to see the reasons why—sometimes with happy results.

Take the case of a company that we financed a few years ago. The operators needed $450,000 which was broken down as follows: $200,000 to repay commercial finance companies, $100,000 to purchase inventories, $100,000 for additional working capital, and $50,000 to purchase additional machinery and equipment.

My company put up $250,000 and secured a $100,000 term loan from a bank. The remaining $100,000 was developed on a revolving line based on accounts receivable.

But this was a very thin deal. The company's net worth was $60,000 and earnings had been averaging less than $15,000 per year after taxes. However, there were some economies inherent in the deal itself which netted out increased interest costs against the savings of discounts on raw materials, savings on freight costs possible because the ability to carry larger inventories meant they could ship by rail in carload lots. These savings netted out to a plus figure of $15,000, an amount by which post-tax profits would increase if operations remained as they had been. This financing worked extremely well. The company realized the projected savings and profitable operations have expanded.

The primary consideration in every favorable recommendation has been the quality of the management. They were believable not so much because of their past earnings record as because of their stability. They had operated their business for 12 years and had succeeded in overcoming the problems they faced. They had been tested in the sense that weaker men might not have had the resiliency and determination to come through. When they showed me their projections I was receptive. The whole picture made sense.

Earlier in this chapter I made a remark that new funds should not go into something new for the company. Small businessmen frequently fail to understand this and are disappointed when their loan application is declined.

How to Raise Money for Your Small Business

When the operators of a company seek to borrow money to get into a new line or diversify, they may get past point number 2 by showing how they will use the funds to the satisfaction of the banker, but they will probably fail at point 3. If the money is earmarked for a new venture, then their ability to make a believable story about the profit-making merits of the proposal depends solely on their demonstrated past performance.

In this case there is one very important proviso, however. Any business, large or small, should not borrow funds for a new venture unless their existing business can support the debt should the new venture prove to be a dud.

Many small businessmen are disappointed when their applications for financing to build a marketing organization are declined. Sometimes they want the new money for advertising. Or to develop a new product. All of these cases fall into the same category, and the essential question is: *Can the business as it is presently constituted support the debt if the new funds are lost.*

In this area small businesses are terrifically handicapped as compared with large companies. A while ago I saw in *The New York Times* that a very large electronics concern has borrowed funds to invest in a new venture. The reason they can do it is that the profits from their established businesses are more than ten times the amount they are borrowing.

One time I made a very bad loan to a company because I forgot this prime rule. It was a service organization selling, installing and servicing highly specialized equipment to industrial accounts. It had done well. Then, over a period of a year, it developed its own line of equipment and adapted it to meet the special requirements of a large group of potential customers. We advanced the company $100,000 based on our favorable assessment of the management, their demonstrated ability to make money, and the *potential* of the new venture.

How to Raise Money for Your Small Business

It did not work out as planned. True enough, the company sold some of their new products and made some profits. But it turned out that the market for their products was characterized by great peaks of demand and large valleys of no demand. During these times of no demand the organization which existed prior to the financing could not support the debt we had advanced. It was a question of either closing the business down or combining it with another company. In the latter case, the other company would have to provide a base from which our client could operate profitably during the time of no demand. Fortunately, we were able to find such another company. But by the time we levelled out and got the new combined operation going smoothly the original $100,000 had increased to nearly $750,000.

We stuck with this company and the company which took it over because the mistake was ours. We also knew that the whole deal made sense provided the problem of sales peaks and valleys could be levelled out by making our client part of something larger so that it did not matter when the sales came in. Luckily, we were able to accomplish our objective.

Every now and then, sticking to your policies can be costly in terms of chances missed. One case in particular comes to mind, and I tell it here only because the reader will probably appreciate learning that big mistakes can be avoided only at the expense of sometimes letting a good deal slip by.

The applicant was a man who had spent his working life as an employee. He had never worked for himself and had never been the manager of his own company. He had developed an idea for a "teaching machine." It was highly complex, brand new in its field, and would sell for over $15,000—and *he had never made a working model.* He needed $300,000 to complete his model and, if it was successful, another $300,000 to build inventory and, hopefully, bring in some sales. More than $250,000 had already been invested in the project when he came to see us. His application met none of our tests, and we declined the opportunity to finance his project on every ground we could think of.

Want to know what happened? The man got his money from a very substantial financial group. His program was completed as he said it would be. His product met with such complete acceptance that he received an offer to sell his company—an offer which he took. The result? Within 20 months the financing group had gotten back its $600,000, with interest, and had as their profit common stock of the acquiring company worth $800,000. Not bad.

These investors were very astute. They still are. But I would turn the same man down again tomorrow. Which brings me to the next point.

Bankers, lenders, investors—everyone wants to know that he will get his money back. In addition, a profit will be very acceptable to them, but the minimum expectation is a recovery of the principal amount of their advances. That is why I would *always* turn down a proposition like the one presented by the man with the teaching machine. No matter how he or anyone in similar circumstances would try, it would be impossible to convince me that I would ever get repaid.

Sometimes, albeit very infrequently, a small businessman can get his money even when his presentation is weak in other areas, provided he has collateral. That is to say, the weaker his picture the better the collateral must be. The lender is looking to get paid.

Collateral is the source of that repayment. Remember the axiom that banks will lend a man anything provided he has U. S. Government bonds as collateral. It is that simple; the lender is making the loan on the strength of the credit of our government. The banker probably doesn't even care what the small business is about. Collateral of this quality makes a lender feel safe and sound, and he won't spend any fitful afternoons ruining his golf game with unpleasant thoughts of a loan gone sour.

How to Raise Money for Your Small Business

This book is not, however, directed to the man who has government bonds as collateral. Most small businesses I have seen got started on a wing and a prayer. If there was any collateral at all the chances are good that it had been used for borrowing purposes at the very start of the business.

Bankers have an old saying that "every loan is a good one the day it is made." Loans get into trouble later—and it is the same thing with small businesses: They all look promising, financially, the day they are started. That is why it is frequently easier to get funds for your business *before* it has started. Since there is no history, no past, you tell your story only about the future of your enterprise.

But when you come in to see a potential lender about financing after your business has a track record, take it from me that the ability to repay the loans will be judged by the demonstrated history of how the company has handled its obligations up to then.

A very important aspect of the potential lenders considerations will be estimating the effect of the previous guideposts I mentioned. The lender will consider the amount of money involved, the use it is to be put to, the likelihood of profits being generated under those circumstances, and thus the likelihood of getting repaid.

Sometimes, as I say, collateral plays the most important part, particularly in a weak situation—but not always. Recently two men in their late thirties came to see us about financing their business. They were supplying contractors with specialized metal parts used in finishing off the interiors of buildings. They had taken over the business when the father of one of them had allowed the business to get into real financial trouble. In effect, they had obtained the resignation of the older man and had set about trying to get the company back on its feet. In the following five years they had reduced the total obligations of the business by more than $1.2 million and when they came to see us there was no long-term debt against the company. They wanted to increase their working capital by borrowing long-term funds. The new money would be used to repay a large part of the short-term money they were borrowing from a factor.

In other words, these two men had operated their business on a basis of paying off an accumulated long-term debt. This had depleted the company of working capital which they had to have to operate. They therefore borrowed the required working capital with the accounts receivable as collateral. Such arrangements are expensive and take much detailed clerical work. Their proposal to us was to re-finance the factor with long-term loans; a program which would reduce interest costs, cut out a lot of clerical detail work involved in daily accounts-receivable financing, and, on their balance sheet, show adequate working capital without actually borrowing, in total, more money than they were borrowing presently.

What was the most important consideration in my favorable recommendation? It was the fact these men had shown what they could do in the way of paying their debts. Their record was excellent. As could be imagined, the other points were adequately covered as well. A company that is paying off its debt is usually one that is being well-managed in other areas.

This is the best type of collateral; the certain knowledge that the borrower can and will pay his debts. It is a company's history of debt-paying that establishes its credit rating in Dun and Bradstreet, for example. Remember this; a lender will regard it as his prime collateral.

I have always felt that lenders should really consider they have failed in an important aspect of their work if they have to go back to the collateral to collect. While the purpose of the collateral is to protect the lender from loss, recourse to the collateral means that something has gone very wrong. At the least it means the borrower cannot meet his obligations as they mature; at the worst that the borrower is bankrupt.

Which brings me to the final point in the check list: *When can you repay the proposed loan?*

How to Raise Money for Your Small Business

It is at this point that a great many men make liars of themselves. At least half the financing proposals I have ever seen have fallen into the trap of giving the appearance of having the ability to repay a loan sooner than could conceivably be possible. It is a mistake that I have made myself, and it is a very serious mistake.

Your request for funds may have passed muster on all other counts. The prospective lender may have accepted your proposition in every way. He may even have accepted your projection of ability to repay. *You have to live with it.* And what happens while you are "living with it" is discouraging in the extreme.

For example, take the mistake I helped to make. I was working for a manufacturing company in Cincinnati. They were in the advertising display business. In the advertising display business the time that money is tied up in a job is relatively short. Indeed, on some jobs I can recall, it was not unusual to take the job, build it, ship it out and bill it to the customer within three weeks. Under these circumstances it was usual that the company would not yet have received invoices from its suppliers. Thus it was not infrequent that the company would have received payment for its work before the invoices from suppliers would be due. The *time span* of the company's working capital turnover was very short.

Under these conditions the company's financial arrangements with its bank were adequate and satisfactory. However, the management decided to branch into the fabrication of training devices for aircraft.

At first, these contracts were similar to the bigger jobs of display in that the time they were in the plant was not long—up to 90 days. Gradually, though, the contracts became larger, more complex, and required a very long time to complete. These were government contracts and the company took advantage of the progress payments available. Under this arrangement, at a 75 per cent rate, for example, the government inspectors assigned to the job estimate the

[41]

per cent of completion of the job each month. The contractor then billed the government an amount equal to 75 per cent of the percentage of completion of the total dollar value of that contract.

My job, among others, was to prepare financial forecasts. Based on the historical experience of the company, these forecasts showed the need for a certain amount of cash and the ability to repay it at a given time. On this basis we arranged for the financing we thought we needed.

Then we began to "live with" my error. My mistake was in not accurately allowing for the "time span" of working capital turnover, so that all the while the company was making reasonable profits on its work, the bank was always on our backs because the company needed the money for nearly three times the length of time I had originally projected. I had very inaccurately calculated the time it would take to complete the jobs.

The banker was entirely correct in keeping on the pressure, however. We had said we would pay the loans off and we could not do it. Finally, we solved the problem another way by using the so-called "retainages" as side collateral for a loan from a commercial finance company and applying the proceeds to the bank loans. ("Retainages" are the 25 per cent amounts which are withheld when the 75 per cent is billed out).

The time it takes to do a given job in a given small business is one way of describing the business itself. In future chapters of this book I will say more about this. Here, as regards setting the time when your loan can be repaid, the important consideration is *not to underestimate*.

If you have applied for and obtained a loan that fits all your needs *except* the ability to pay it back as agreed, you may well come to regret ever taking the money in the first place.

Take the case of a small appliance manufacturer who came to see us. He had originally financed his operation on a basis where his terms of sale to the type of customers he then had allowed him to turn his working capital every 90 days. That is to say, every 90 days he would receive from his customers payments based on sales which equalled the amounts of money he had tied up in accounts receivable and inventories. These funds he would then use to pay the wages, overhead and material costs which were incurred in making the merchandise in the first place; what was left was his profit.

On this basis his business grew modestly and profitably. His profits were sufficient to provide the extra working capital needed to support the extra sales. His was a well-balanced, small manufacturing company that was growing out of retained earnings. Anyone would have financed this operator.

And someone did. The company had the chance to acquire the business of another company whose product line was completely complementary with the existing lines as regards customers, methods of distribution and marketing, packaging and the like. But the new lines were dissimilar as regards manufacturing cycles and, therefore, so was the "time span" of the working capital required. The new lines took much longer to be made. Inventory requirements were greater because of a wider number of items in the line and the necessity of carrying a complete line. Nevertheless, the operator purchased the business at a good price, not realizing this important fact.

The lender was at fault here too. It is a lender's job to know and understand the nature of money and to comprehend the time span of its use. Unfortunately, too many lenders look only at the credit—at the balance sheet and earnings history—in making their judgements. And that is what was done here.

The newly acquired lines became a drag on the business within 90 days. To assist with growing cash needs the operator went back to the lender to get more money. This frightened the lender who then not only would not give more money but insisted on collateral for his existing loans. In the meantime, thanks to an aggressive sales manager hired by the operator when he took over the new lines, sales of all the company's products increased dramatically.

But now, with the company's history of slow payment, suppliers began holding up on shipments of parts and raw materials. This forced the company to be late in its deliveries, and in order to get products finished as quickly as possible once materials were on hand, quality was sacrificed. One large shipment went out to a good customer which contained defective parts in every appliance. The order came back, and that customer began purchasing elsewhere.

Now the lender was really worried and called the operator in "for a little talk." That meant the loans were called and the operator was told to pay off the loans as soon as possible, but in no event later than three months.

That is when he came to see me. I wish the story had a happy ending, but it did not. I went over the company's problem and the operator and I agreed as to the difficulty he had. We went to see the lender, who would not move one inch from his position. In order to adequately refinance this small business, enough fresh cash was necessary to pay off the existing lender, take care of the suppliers, who by this time were getting paid in 120 days or longer, provide the operation with enough additional cash to support the longer time span required of the new lines added and start a new marketing program to get back the customers lost during the previous 12 months while the business was having its problems.

It would have been cheaper to start all over again. In any case, we declined the offering. The operator tried desperately to get some financing, and when he could not his business failed. It was sold at auction to satisfy the secured interest of the lender who had put up the money for the acquisition. The operator lost everything.

How to Raise Money for Your Small Business

Yet this business was a good business. It always showed profits. Because of the time span of the money required in the new lines, and because this was not accurately comprehended and provided for, eventually the company could not pay its bills. When that happens you're broke. Bankers call it being unliquid. It still means the same; you're broke.

So far in this chapter I have tried to point out five of the essential ingredients necessary if your proposal for financing is to meet with success. And the examples described should give something of the "flavor" of how the condition of your small business provides the underlying foundations of your presentation.

When you are presenting your proposal to the prospective lender or investor, you must be aware of his particular requirements as to answering the question, "When can you repay the loan?"

Banks traditionally loan funds that can be completely repaid at least once a year. Such loans are made, for example, for the purposes of allowing a store to carry a Christmas inventory; the funds are borrowed in October to make purchases and then repaid in February from sales made over the holidays. Banks, you must remember, have developed this pattern because they rely on demand deposits for the source of funds they lend. A demand deposit is the type of deposit one makes in his personal checking account; the money is deposited at the bank subject to one's demand for it by writing a check. The theory is that, since the depositors' funds are on demand, any loans should be for a short period only, thus avoiding the possibility of a situation where the depositors want their funds and the bank does not have enough on hand to meet the demands.

During the Second World War, banks made many longer term loans of up to three and sometimes five years. The government provided various schemes to keep the banks from facing a situation of excess demands against deposits. One such program was the "V" loans, and there were others.

How to Raise Money for Your Small Business

With this experience, however, banks became more readily willing to grant loans of more than a year, and, today, a three-year bank loan is not uncommon. But banks still prefer the shortest term possible, and the small businessman will do well to remember this important fact.

On the other hand, a company such as mine is not interested in a loan of less than five years; usually the term is ten years. That is because the nature of its business is intentionally focused in that direction. The small businessman who needs short-term funds is as uninteresting a prospect to me as the long-term borrower is to a bank. That is why it is of the utmost importance for the borrower to seek out the type of lender who specializes in the type of financing required.

There is one more mistake that is common among small businessmen. If they say, "I want to borrow $10,000 for my business and I can repay at the rate of $1,000 per month," they become immediately suspect to me. Such men have probably been used to borrowing money for personal uses where that type of repayment program is the accepted standard. But for business, the same rules do not apply. His personal ability to repay should have very little bearing on his company's ability to repay. Remember that the financing you are seeking is *for your small business*. You, as the principal at interest in your small business, will be expected to guarantee payment of the loans, so your personal ability to repay has some importance as a side consideration to the lender. But, as I have said, I believe a lender has failed when he has to resort to the collateral on side security to collect his loans. Therefore, program the loan repayment schedule to fit the company's ability, nothing else.

It would be inaccurate to suggest that this is the only way to successfully solicit your financing. I can promise, however, that if your presentation factually and objectively deals with the five points, you will be 90 per cent of the way towards your loan.

The remaining 10 per cent of the way is going to be

strictly between you and the lender. This is going to be a relationship on the basis of one-to-one. Think of it this way: Although your loan may be made by the "X" National Bank, it will really be Mr. "Z" of the bank that makes the deal. This is where personalities come in.

In your community there are probably a half-dozen lenders of various kinds. Each of these lenders will have a different attitude and a different style. *Do not* apply for your financing until you have taken the time to find out what the attitudes and "styles" of each potential lender are and until you have decided which one suits the type of business you are running. Then, get to know some of the lending officers of the place you select to determine if you can find someone you "feel at home with," someone whose individual style seems to match your own.

This is the man to see. If you have selected properly, this man will be working in an organization that has specialized in your type of situation and he will be sympathetic to you personally.

Now your job is 95 per cent complete. The last thing you must do is to present *yourself* as the best possible collateral for your loan. After all, in the final analysis, the success of your business will depend on you; hence the success of any loans you may receive will likewise depend on you.

Personally, I never ask anyone to take the medicine that I have not already taken. When I went to work for the First SBIC of New Jersey, the company was new, it had no real history of earnings and much was left to be done. My boss and I agreed on what the company could afford to pay its full-time general manager and I agreed to work for those wages, even though the amount was nearly half what I had been making. Our understanding and my acceptance was based on fact. We expected the small businessmen who came to us for financing to be living within their means. How could we insist on that if we ourselves did not live within ours.

What did this mean to me and my family? When we

moved to South Orange we bought a less expensive house than the one we had had. I sold my sports car; it was a Ferrari 250 GT, bright red with red leather inside; it would exceed 150 miles per hour, and it broke my heart to sell it. We resigned from our clubs. My wife gave up her maid, etc. I won't say it was fun but it was worthwhile. In any case, we did the things we had to do.

The point cannot be overemphasized. The subjective opinion of one man for another is nowhere more influential than where money is concerned. Spoken of in general terms, this is referred to as "credit." What is meant is "credibility"—belief in the other man.

It may surprise you to know that all transactions on the major stock exchanges are done on a "credit" basis. The gross amount of dollars which changes hands in the course of a day on the New York Stock Exchange is a staggering average of 300 million—all on the mutual trust the members have for one another, the "credibility" of their fellows.

There is a proposal on my desk today to provide financing for a worthwhile project. The presentation meets or exceeds most of the standards of acceptability. It fails because I cannot bring myself to believe the man who has prepared it. In these cases I ask an associate to check the proposal without telling him why just to see if he gets the same feeling. Most of the time, if a man affects another negatively, as in this case, he will affect most other men negatively.

What is there about this man and his story that doesn't ring true? Some political writers might call it "dialectic materialism"—saying something that conveys a meaning different from the truth, while the statement itself is not false.

My favorite example of this concerns the running of a horse race and how it was later reported. The story goes that at one of the International Stakes—at Bowie, Maryland—many of the major European, Asian and American countries had sent their finest race horses. These were to run a stakes race for the international championship. Shortly before the race an influenza virus attacked the stables and all but the American and Russian entries were scratched on account of sickness. The race was duly held and the American horse won by a length and a half.

The account of the race in the Russian Press went something like this:

> Out of an original field of 10 of the world's finest horses, the race was run in record time. The Russian entry finished a strong second and was closing in on the leader at the finish. The American horse ran next to last.

The account is not a lie, but it is also not the truth, because it does not accurately convey the actual happening, to say the least!

The proposal before me falls prey to the same conditions. We have checked its accuracy and are satisfied. Yet, it was presented to show as highly a slanted position as the horse race quotation showed. In short, I do not believe the man who prepared the proposal. I believe this man would take the truth and manipulate it to serve whatever convenience happens to be his objective at the moment. In the money business, this suspicion is enough to effectively kill any possibility of a deal.

One time a man came in for an interview concerning a loan for his company. It was a struggling company that had a faint air of hope of prosperity connected with it and we undertook to work up a financing proposal. During the course of our investigation we found the man would always change the subject each time we would ask him about himself and his personal background. This tended to make us that much more curious.

It finally transpired the man had been in jail when he was much younger. The thought that this fact would keep him from securing financing if it were known had led him to change his name and move from that part of the country where he had been living. Perhaps this fact would have made the difference to some people, but it made not the slightest difference to me. The man had lived down his past and had demonstrated his ability to build a proper and stable life for himself and his family.

There are many examples of how this subjective feeling creeps into the over-all business judgement concerning a loan. I trust the reader will not miss the point. A small businessman is his own best collateral, or his own poorest collateral, depending on the facts.

You can expect the prospective lender will look at your personal life with close attention. If it does not substantiate the picture and impression you wish to convey about your business, then you may well be disappointed in your attempts to get that loan.

Sometimes a small businessman will raise equity capital instead of getting a loan. If that is the program, then very much the same situations will be present. The investor will be interested in the same patterns as the lender. He will want to know the same general information and he will be interested in the development of a program in the same way as the lender.

But with one proviso—the quality will have to be many times better to attract the equity investor. Remember, an equity investor can buy General Motors or Proctor and Gamble stocks as an alternative to investing in the small business. As a rule, your company should show a consistent earnings picture for a minimum of three years. All debt should have been handled as agreed and the debt should not be more than three times the amount of equity capital.

Most small businesses do not qualify for equity financing. Those that do qualify probably would not accept it. The reason is very simple; the small businessman who has built up his business to the point where it can qualify for equity financing will probably not want to sell the results of his sweat and toil. For that is what one does when one brings in an investor—one sells a part of the equity to the investor.

How to Raise Money for Your Small Business

The same program is true if you are trying to get an underwriter interested in doing a "public deal," as it is called. Here the quality must be very much greater than when soliciting funds from a private investor. But, again, the same rules apply and your performance must meet the same general tests. When a small business reaches the stage of interesting an underwriter, then it has truly arrived.

The spate of failures of companies underwritten, companies that "went public," during the early 1960–1961 period, can be attributed to one simple fact. Underwriters are human just like other people. They had customers who were willing to buy new issues of stocks. Therefore they looked around for companies to underwrite, and they looked in some very dark corners. Most of the underwritings that were done during this time were for companies that under no circumstances should have even been considered for this type of financing. But money was plentiful, there were buyers and the underwriters wanted to make money. And why not? If you were a small businessman, why not take the money while you could?

The companies thus financed have, as a rule, done nothing creative or even profitable with the funds provided. The stock market slump of 1962–1963 wiped out the values of most of the small business stocks and it is only very recently that the stock market has begun to pay them much attention.

In conclusion, financing your small business is an important aspect of your work as its operator or one of its operators. If you follow the guidelines I have mentioned you should be successful. At the least, you will avoid the most frequent mistakes characteristic of small businessmen. Remember the questions that will be asked:

1) How much money do you need?
2) How are you going to use it?
3) Will your business make more money?
4) Will the bank be repaid?
5) And when will that be?

And, most important, remember that a man and the small business he operates needs a "credit" rating—the impression of "credibility," based on past performance, which expresses one man's measure of another.

Let me close this chapter with an observation that may be helpful and is certainly significant. I have never seen, nor have I ever heard of, a small business being formed by a man whose expertise was financial. Small businesses are formed by men who are engineers, salesmen, production specialists; in my experience not one has been founded by an expert in finance.

3

How to Get Customers

Believe me when I say that if it were possible to give the definitive answer to the problem posed in the title of this chapter, there would be little else left in the business world that could remain unconquered before my onslaught. I do not know how to get customers, except in a general way, so what I mean to discuss here might be more appropriately called, *How to get customers you can afford*. Perhaps that should have been the title of this chapter. Anyway, judge for yourself after you have read it.

Customers, as a class, are worthy of some general comment. You can have the best products in the world, you can have all the financing you will ever need, you can have the most modern and up-to-date, completely equipped plant, you can have the smartest people in the world working for you, but until you get a customer you haven't got a business.

A business, large or small, exists only as it relates to its customer or customers. The customer can be thought of as the "need" that your business is going to "satisfy." Particularly in small business, the type of customer to be served, the type of need to be satisfied, can be said to determine much about the business and much about the problems it will have.

As a matter of fact, a small business has a pretty good

How to Get Customers

chance for success if it has only the "right" kind of customers and very little else. And it will almost certainly fail if its customers are the "wrong" kind. But always bear this in mind: *You cannot think of your product without thinking of your customer.* Your product can most easily be described in terms of the customers you have or are trying to reach. The same, of course, applies to the other side of the coin: *Your company's relationships with its customers can be best expressed by describing the products the customers buy.* With this as a starting point, let me pass on some observations I have made about the marketing aspects of small business.

First, it is axiomatic with me that if a small business has, along with all the other problems it will face, the problem of *developing the market for its product,* then that small business will eventually fail in one way or another. There is a corollary to this: *A small business will fail if it must continuously fight the technological superannuation of its product.*

What does this mean?

It means that the small business has picked the "wrong" customers. They are "wrong" because:

1) They have to be convinced to do something differently (the small businessman has to develop the market), or

2) They have to be continuously served with newer, more refined or advanced products. (To avoid being "old hat" the small businessman must always update his product.)

I know that what I have just said will be unpopular, particularly because many small businesses are formed by engineers who have developed a product that is, as they say, "at the state of the art." What they mean is that the product is representative of the most advanced techniques and processes and that the product does its work with the greatest accuracy, reliability, speed or what have you.

Usually, when a small business starts off on this basis, the products are characterised by both "wrong" points; their technical nature subjects them to becoming technically obsolete and usually also means that the customers have to be

How to Get Customers

developed, in the sense that they require training or educating of some kind to use the products.

An excellent example is the case of the three engineers I have mentioned several times in other connections. Their product line was devoted to highly complex computers which they designed and manufactured. These computers were apparently not too bad in certain applications. However, the potential users had to substantially change the way they were doing things in order to make use of the high speed and other qualities of these computers. Quite naturally, sales projections were based on a so-called market survey and were, in that sense, very modest. What was unknown was the *cost of selling*, in time and money, which was necessary to get a potential user to switch over to the company's products. This one fact alone was sufficient for me to predict the demise of that venture. As might be expected, a group of men who did that job of planning so poorly were also poor in other areas, so that the death knell was sounded even earlier.

Actually, to be completely fair, this company did not fail in the sense of a total cessation of activity. A much larger company bought the assets at the bankruptcy sale and has made a good success of the product line. It was able to do this because it could afford to take the time to do the proper selling job and had the funds to put into it.

The appeal of a product is tremendous when it provides a better way of doing something. The pay-off for success of this type of product is higher than any other. The risk of loss is also the greatest. The man who had developed the so-called "teaching machine" is a classic case. He was successful and in a short time was a millionaire.

But remember this when you are thinking about your small business. There is a "balance" to things in the business world. If what you propose to do is along the lines of the teaching machine, you must be prepared to face the high odds of failure. The "balance" in these cases comes from the large premium placed on success. The greater the risk of loss, the greater will be the chance of gain.

One of the finest characteristics of our American economy is the art of competitiveness which results in better products. Most of these products are the result of work by the larger corporations—or at least by the time these products reach the customer in volume they are part of a large company. It has to be that way. A large company does its development work out of the profits of its established business. A small company has to do its development work out of funds from other sources (usually borrowed) and cannot afford to keep up.

One time we were asked to finance a company that made power supplies—the standard electronic components that regulate, alter and transmit power. They are found everywhere; for example, every TV set has them.

This company, however, made very specialized power supplies. The finished unit was about the size of a carton of cigarettes, weighed about 3 pounds and sold for $35,000. The units were used in connection with our government's space program, and certain types of rockets required several of these units.

The company had used borrowed funds to supplement the original capital in developing this product. They had orders on hand and were making profits on shipments. The proposal was for my company to provide cash for the development of another type of power supply.

We declined, basing our decision on the likelihood that the existing products would be subject to technological superannuation long before the new proposed products would be profitable. This would both delay the development of the new product while work was done to bring the old products up to date and use up the funds allocated and provided for the new products in rescuing the old. The inevitable end of this company was brought about when that very thing happened. A large electronics firm developed a method of making the same power supply lighter, smaller and more reliable.

This, then, is the first guideline in thinking about the customers (and products) your small business will have:

Your small size will limit you to modest engineering or product development expense, thereby limiting you to products which do not, by their nature, require heavy engineering and development expense.

Take also the case of the company that developed the teaching machine. When the operator of this business sold out, he undoubtedly recognized an important fact. Since he had created a tremendous debt in developing his product line, he could almost certainly not expect to find adequate financing for the expensive marketing program which was, at that point, necessary to get the customers—schools, colleges, etc.—to allocate funds for the purchase of the equipment. By selling out at the time he did, this operator was recognizing the necessity of then obtaining many times as much money as was required to develop the product in order to market it effectively.

This is the second guideline:

Your small size will limit you to modest marketing expenditures, thereby confining the product-customer relationship to things which do not involve high marketing expenditures of a developmental nature.

I have never seen a sales projection prepared by a small company that forecast a decline in sales, and I have often thought this might be indicative of something. About the only conclusion that seems to be valid in most instances is that the sales projections are prepared by small businessmen and they, taken as a class of people, are optimistic to say the least.

Optimism never was responsible for increasing sales. On the contrary, it has frequently resulted in the gradual

How to Get Customers

build-up of a sense of complacency on the part of the small business operator, a condition that can lead straight to disaster.

Two men sat across my desk one day about three years ago and presented a proposal to buy a company. They were salesmen from another company which was a direct competitor of the one they wanted to buy. Their record of selling with their present employer was excellent. They clearly knew the market. Moreover, they seemed to be individuals who were aware of what it was going to take to get their proposal off the ground. Of the total purchase price of $350,000, they could provide almost $200,000. They had saved $150,000 over the years between them and could get the rest by selling their houses and moving into apartments. They fit the financial tests.

The company they planned to buy had been rocking along as the owner had gotten older, and sales were declining. The proposal the men had prepared showed a turn-around in the sales the first year and dramatic increases each year after that.

In the discussions we had, which extended over several weeks, it became apparent that to meet the financial burdens they were undertaking, the sales increases would have to be right on the nose as projected. If they fell down, the resulting cash flow deficiency would require that additional funds would have to be put into the business to meet current obligations.

The men absolutely believed in their ability to get these sales increases. They showed market surveys which indicated an increase in the market of 8 per cent per year. The increases in their projected sales were 25 per cent per year. To me this meant that they would have to obtain the difference of 17 per cent by *taking business away from their competitors*. The men also believed they could accomplish this and they assured me they "could bring a lot of accounts with them."

How to Get Customers

We made the financing. The men purchased the business. They did not even come close to their projections.

We stayed with them, however, out of a conviction that *given some time* these two men could expand their business faster than the market was increasing. We bought the men this time by refinancing their debt on a longer term basis and providing fresh cash from time to time.

Guideline number three is:

If your sales projection shows increases above the general market increases, they will come from accounts you take away from competitors. Be prepared to find that this always takes longer and costs more than you expect simply because competitors do not like to lose their accounts. Your small size will limit the amount of time and money you can allocate to this task.

I want now to speak of a special way to think about a small business that is most useful and informative. I cannot overemphasize the accuracy of the insights that I have gained from including this in my analysis of small businesses. Later on, in other chapters, I will have more to say about this, but for now I will mention only its application to the sales aspect of a small business. Although I did not originate the theory, I believe it will assist many small businessmen in getting a better understanding of their operation.

Businesses can be divided into three groups according to the complexity of their relationships with their customers. Many small businesses start off as a so-called "job shop." In this, the simplest type of operation, the small business may manufacture its products upon receipt of a customer order. It might be a service type of operation such as a dry cleaner or an auto body shop. There, when work is brought in, the small business starts up its machinery or uses its tools to complete the work. In this type of operation, the needs of the customers are satisfied by the equipment and personnel of the small business on a "per job" basis, hence the term "job shop."

How to Get Customers

This is the simplest type of business in terms of the marketing requirements. There is much flexibility and "custom" work. It is an appropriate type of organization for small business just because it is so flexible and because it can serve customer needs on a "custom" basis.

The type of business operation that is considered to be on the next level of complexity is characterized by an end product which is the sum of many component parts. As regards marketing, at this level a company has some flexibility left to serve its customers but usually will have more end products in its line. The relationship with the customer at this level is based on the company's having a family of products with which it hopes to get the business. The company's ability to provide "custom" work is greatly reduced and flexibility is likewise very much more limited.

A small business that would fit into this category might manufacture small power hand tools, or make a line of furniture, or package a line of food products such as jellies and jams.

Here, a small business is more committed to a given product than is the much simpler job shop. The operator has, of necessity, done much product planning. He has had to provide for the acquisition of a number of raw materials and component parts. His inventories will reflect large amounts of various merchandise.

The operator on this level must engage in a more complex and larger marketing operation than at the job shop level. Now there must be regular production scheduled into some kind of warehousing or storage facility. From there finished products are ordered out to the customer in shipments of various amounts. As compared with the job shop, this level of operation requires that inventory be made against future orders, not upon the receipt of an order.

Finally, the third level is reached. This level is characterized by a method of production that is geared to turn out a given amount of finished product in a given time. An exam-

How to Get Customers

ple would be a refinery where the process of making gasoline was set up; another example might be a chemical plant making chlorine.

The marketing point here is that such a process-type of operation usually totally eliminates product flexibility. A plant that is set up to make gasoline might be adjusted to make kerosene, but it could never make chlorine. And this type of operation requires that it be run at a given speed, at which it will make a given amount of product. Usually such process-type plants can be run at only one speed—their design speed.

Now the customer relationships are even more restricted. The customer is offered only one product, and enough customers must be found to take the production. The marketing program here must be completed and a commitment made by management *before the factory is even built.*

There will be a good deal more said about these three "levels" or types of business operations later on. But as regards customers, they give us guideline number four:

Your small size will have much to do with determining the type of products you can offer your customers; hence the type of customers you should solicit should be capable of being serviced within the limitations of a product line that you can afford to make.

Here are a few cases illustrative of the various levels described above.

A typical job shop operation was the advertising display business we did in Cincinnati. I have already pointed out the financial arrangements—we turned over our working capital very quickly. In the advertising display business a salesman calls on the customer and works out a design for the display. The order is brought into the plant where the materials are purchased and the labor and equipment are provided. The order is produced and shipped. That is the cycle. For all intents and purposes that customer will have to be sold again if he is to buy again. The product, in this case an advertising display, will very likely never be made again. It was a one-time job.

As regards the customer, he looked at it the same way. He would very probably never order the same job again. He might buy from the company again, but that would depend on service, its ability to design and fabricate what he wanted, and delivery. For the customer, too, it was a one-job-at-a-time relationship.

The next level of complexity is well described by a metal stamping operation with which I am familiar. The two owners came to see us four years ago. At that time they had a small, moderately profitable stamping business which catered to a job-shop type of customer. They had good machinery and excellent tool makers and were making slow but steady progress. They needed money to purchase a business in the stamping field, and we gave it to them.

But what made sense to me was their long-range objective. They had gotten into the lighting-fixture business and were selling basic stampings to several of the lighting-fixture houses. The fixture houses would plate, polish and wire-up the stampings to make all manner of home lighting products.

This is what they had observed: There were a number of small stamping operations that were only marginally successful. The fixture houses had to purchase parts for their lamps from several stamping operators because the tooling happened to be located in various places and was so expensive to duplicate that one supplier could not afford to do the tooling for any one job. The cost could not be recovered.

This is what they proposed: They would need a continuing financial commitment. With this, they could pick up small stamping operations as they became available; the tooling they would thus acquire would supplement the lighting-fixture business. They would then use some more of the commitment to re-work the tooling so that parts made from it would be compatible with all other parts in the line. They reasoned that the ability to provide a complete line

How to Get Customers

would entitle them *to get the customers they wanted away from their competitors.*

Their proposal was really a marketing plan to give them a competitive advantage. The men had correctly identified the conditions they would have to control before this advantage would be workable. We gave them the commitment.

Over the ensuing four years, they have acquired a half-dozen or so small operations. They have obtained tooling from other sources as well. This tooling has been re-worked so that all parts fit together where required. And, *they have increased sales more than twice as much as the market has expanded.*

The relationship between this company and its customers now is a classic case of the "second level" operation. The customers need a great variety of component parts which fit together to make the basic metal part of a lighting fixture. Since the company has been able to acquire the necessary tooling to supply its customers with a complete line of parts, the customers can deal with one supplier instead of several.

Here was a situation where the company wanted to increase its business with certain customers. There was, as you can see, much work that preceeded their ability to do so.

The third level, or process-type of product-customer relationship, was well shown in a situation that developed in a company that, fortunately, we had nothing to do with. This operation was started by a man who had made a great deal of money in a business he had built up and then sold to a large national concern. He put most of this money into a chemical manufacturing plant.

He had the contacts—the customers—from his past years in a related business. His sales projections were very optimistic and showed a heavy requirement for plant and equipment to produce the chemicals.

To make a long story short, the plant was built and turned "on stream." The chemicals that were produced were of good quality. But the orders did not materialize as planned and

How to Get Customers

the plant was forced to run at less than 50 per cent of capacity. At this level, the losses were staggering.

But the man kept plugging away. Suddenly, several large users became customers. Now, at that point, the plant could not produce the volume required to meet sales orders taken!

It takes a year to build a chemical plant of the kind required and get it running efficiently. The man was forced to buy product from competitors to fill his orders and keep his customers while he was raising money to build another plant. He finally got the money but by then his sales volume was so great that the plant he had designed did not have sufficient capacity to meet the demands. The financial backers dropped out at this point and the business failed.

This was a case where the type of customers the man proposed to sell had certain characteristic patterns of behavior regarding their suppliers. It made no difference that the operator was adequately financed at the start, that his quality was good or that his plant was new and efficient. Because of the demands made by the customers he was serving, he was forced to operate his one facility at a loss because of low volume and then later to buy from competitors because his facility was inadequate because of high volume.

The types of customers a small businessman attempts to sell had better be ones he can live with. Customers can sometimes be the downfall of a small business that has done everything else correctly.

There will be more said about these three levels of a business later on. In summary, there is a very close relationship between your customers and your product. Be very sure you have correctly identified this relationship from the customers' point of view and have furnished your product with adequate characteristics and qualities to satisfy the customers' needs.

Pricing is a vital part of any company's relations with its customers and is especially important when the seller is a small business. In pricing his product a small businessman

How to Get Customers

faces decisions in two areas as regards his ability to make a sale *because of the price* and one area as regards his ability to make a sale *in spite of the price.*

Take the first decision area, and this case where price was the controlling ingredient in the failure of a small business. The company manufactured a line of electrical contractors' supplies including rigid steel conduit. That is a standard item in which all suppliers have very much the same product and sales are made on the basis of price and delivery and in some cases on the basis of personal relationships between the salesman and the buyer.

In this case, the manufacturer had established his business after a very impressive career in sales management for a large national concern. He had applied to my firm for financing to provide his company with modern machinery, semi-automated, which would reduce his costs substantially. At the time he applied for this financing he was manufacturing his own lines of several products in his field but was purchasing his rigid steel conduit under a contract from an established supplier. The new machinery would allow the company to buy the raw pipe directly from the steel mills and to fabricate it into rigid steel conduit. The cost to the company of products thus furnished would be nearly 25 per cent less than costs under the purchase contract. This cost saving would be sufficient in total dollars to pay for the machinery over a very acceptable 24 months, and profits were forecast to be handsome.

We arranged the financing and the equipment was ordered.

At about this time, the market price of rigid steel conduit began to decline. Very shortly the company was losing money on each sale. For example, at the beginning the purchase contract called for a cost of, say, 90 cents. The company then sold this product for $1, just barely managing to get back its overhead and selling costs and a very small profit at best.

With the price deterioration, the company was still purchasing for 90 cents, but was now selling for 80 cents. Prices further declined until, at the bottom, the selling price was 67 cents.

During this time, the new machinery was being rushed to completion. But it was too late. The immense losses the company sustained exhausted its capital before any rigid steel conduit could be made on the new machinery.

It might be asked why the company continued to sell a product on which it was losing such great amounts. This question was asked more than once in various meetings that were held at the company, and always the decision reached was that to stop selling would result in the loss of customers, thereby making more difficult the job of getting sales for the production of the new machinery once it was running and producing. On the other hand, if no sales were made, losses from that area would be stopped. However, the other products the company made were sold in conjunction with rigid steel conduit and it was thought that to cease sales of that line would drastically reduce sales of the related lines, resulting in an over-all loss to the company greater than the loss being sustained in the conduit line alone when offset by profits from the related lines.

In any case, here was the perfect instance where a small business was driven under by a decline in price on its major product.

Guideline number five is:

Your small size will be a great disadvantage if your product line is subject to price declines beyond your control. Smaller size means less capital and thus the time when you have exhausted your ability to sustain a price decline comes more quickly.

I mentioned two areas of selling because of price. The other one is the opposite of the example just given. There are cases where *a sale cannot be made at any price*. And here again being small is a hindrance to corrective action.

At one time I was associated with a group that had many

How to Get Customers

investments. One of them was a soft-drink franchise bottling works in a heavy industrial area of the midwest. As a matter of fact, these men had purchased the business largely on my recommendation. It was one of the worst recommendations I ever have made and they eventually discharged me for it—quite properly so, I might add.

In any event, we wanted to sell our bottled soft drinks in the company cafeterias of a large steel mill. The volume was very attractive and the costs of servicing such a location were low because the route drivers could handle a large number of cases at one central stop. The steel company had contracted the management of its cafeterias to a national concern that specialized in that type of service contract.

We approached the service company with a program. They examined it and said they were not interested. We assumed it was because of price. We submitted again at a lower price. The results were the same. A third time we submitted our bid, and again the answer was "no." At this point our price was so low that we had to abandon the idea.

Several years later I met the same man with whom we had been dealing. He had been promoted to the national home office and I was working for a company that used his company's food services. Under this changed set of circumstances I asked him what had been the real story back in the soft-drink proposal days. His answer was simple and direct. He was buying from a company that supplied many more items and services than we did. Since it was good business for him to buy from the fewest possible sources consistent with quality, etc., he was unwilling to take the soft-drink part of the over-all business away from his supplier merely because we were willing to cut prices.

Guide line number six:

There are many circumstances where you cannot make a sale at any price. Usually this is because of wider considerations such as other products on tie-in deals, delivery, quantity, etc. Your small size will limit you in dealing with this problem area because you will have a smaller product line.

Happily there are many cases where the small size of a business need not put it in the way of the above two pitfalls. These are the cases where the product line of the small business is sold on a basis where price is determined by factors other than cost.

One of the greatest attributes a small businessman can have is the courage to price his product. I don't see it too often, but when a small businessman gets hold of the right product and prices it properly the results are phenomenal.

The small business we financed for the engineer and the accountant is a case in point. The product on which this business was based is a piece of equipment known in the trade as an "automatic machine monitor." It is a device which is attached to a machine, such as a stamping machine or a transfer press, and "monitors" its performance.

That is to say, the device has various electrical circuits which "sense" or "feel" if all the operations have been completed for any given cycle of production. If that is the case, the monitor allows the machine to go through another cycle. If at any time the cycle is not completed, the monitor will automatically shut off the machine and ring a bell for the operator to come and see what happened.

In one shop where these units had been installed, the savings were fantastic. This was an operation consisting of ten transfer presses making metal parts for pencils, pens, etc. Before the installation of the devices, there was a lady operator at each machine watching each cycle with her hand on the "stop" button if anything should go amiss. Since it is very demanding work, each operator required 15 minutes every hour for rest. Thus, they required 15 ladies to run the ten machines.

After the installation of the devices, there were no ladies required at all and production was increased by raising the number of cycles per minute of the presses to a speed that no human being could handle very easily.

How to Get Customers

The manufacturer of the devices, the company we had financed, was pricing these machines based on cost plus profit. It became apparent, however, that the customer could be sold at a *price which he could afford based on his savings*. This price was nearly ten times the prices based on the company's costs.

Prices were raised over a six-month period. Sales *increased* somewhat, partly due, I believe, to the more logical relationship between the promises made for the devices and the higher costs quoted. Apparently some customers had felt the devices could not be that good and still cost so little. But the point of the story is in the ability of the company to price its product based on a *value to the buyer* which had nothing whatever to do with the product's cost.

There are many other products which lend themselves to this type of pricing. In these cases the general price levels may be well established in the market, but they will have been established by the operator's asking, "*What is it worth to the purchaser?*"

An example, and of particular interest to small business, is the cosmetics industry. The price a woman will pay for a lipstick is not related to what it costs to make it. The same is true of a fine restaurant. A steak dinner costs so much to serve. More elegant surroundings add some additional expense, but the customers are willing to pay much more because *that's what they want*.

Generally speaking, I have observed a much higher incidence of success in small businesses that have been able to build this feature into their product line.

Guideline number seven is:

It is particularly important for a small business to have a product line that can be priced on some basis other than cost. The customer relationship is then based on value to him, not on cost to the small business.

There is one cardinal rule in business that can sometimes cause such a strain in a company's relationship with its customers that the customer is lost. That circumstance develops when a customer won't pay his bill.

Nobody likes to pay, but it's a basic essential in business and particularly in small business where one credit loss can spell the end of the company at worst and at the least wipe out the profits from many months of sales. A small business cannot afford a customer who will not pay. That goes for any small business.

One time I had been asked to attend a meeting of the creditors of a manufacturing company that had gone bad in a big way. Most of the trade suppliers were to be there and the company's investors as well. I was asked to come because from time to time I have been able to figure out a way of putting up some fresh cash to save such situations from bankruptcy.

The meeting was held in a large conference room of the subject company's plant location. I just happened to sit across the table from a distinguished-looking older man whose name and connection I did not know. Nor could I guess why this man was there. At a break in the deliberations I asked the company's president who the man was. It turned out he was a trustee for a large, old, and very wealthy Boston estate.

All through the morning, as the terrible tale of mismanagement, poor planning, worse execution and awful results was unfolded, I watched this man. His face would become pale and he would shrink into his seat. Then again, his eyes would get fire in them and he would sit very erect, paying close attention.

Finally, there was another break. During the hiatus I looked over at this gentlemen and said, "If you wouldn't mind, would you tell me how your people ever got into such a bag of worms as this?"

He looked at me for perhaps 15 seconds, then he placed both his hands on the table in front of him and seemed to push himself up out of his chair. He wore pince-nez glasses

How to Get Customers

and as his head trembled they fell off his nose and dangled on the black string which was tied to his coat pocket. His face got quite red and he said, "Yes, young man. I'll tell you." Here he trembled, really quivered, even more. "*Greed!*" he said, and sat down as if all the breath had been knocked out of him.

Take also the case of a company which manufactured a home toilet article product. They were struggling along and finding the competition very rough. Sales were coming in very slowly and, although the company was making money, the owner-manager was getting more and more discouraged.

Then one day he called on a company that was selling products compatible but not competitive with his on a door-to-door sales program. This was a new company and they were very ambitious. A deal was soon made under which the direct sales organization would take a high volume of products from the small manufacturer. The discouragement suddenly vanished from the manufacturer and all efforts were turned to getting out the volume required by the selling organization.

The first orders were shipped in February. The new business to the direct sales outfit was, by itself, three times the volume of all other existing accounts. The manufacturer had made up special packages, increased his production staff and gone to a two-shift basis. Prosperity seemed at hand.

Shipments were made in March and April. However, by the end of April the manufacturer had yet to see the first payment on account from the direct sales organization. By May the manufacturer had exhausted his cash and could not meet the payroll. Conversations with the sales company had been useless. The manufacturer was able to keep his doors open only because his employees knew him to be so honorable they were willing to trust him for their wages.

The manufacturer then made the first real investigation of his customer. He found they were themselves bankrupt and were operating under bankruptcy arrangements at the time

How to Get Customers

he started to ship to them. The operators of the business had a terrible history of being very sharp traders who had previously stuck creditors for large amounts. There was no chance of collecting a dime. The small manufacturer himself immediately went into bankruptcy. (As a measure of the quality of this man, you should know that in three years he had worked his way out of the hole and had made good on all his obligations.)

When a small business—or any business—makes a sale, that sale is *not complete until the money has been paid*. There are, of course, circumstances under which a man will go along with someone who is in trouble. As a matter of fact, properly explained, it is not at all unusual for one company to give special terms to another company that is having some sort of difficulty.

However, once the terms have been agreed upon, including any special terms which may be designed to assist the debtor, that should be the end of it.

When your customer will not pay, close the matter there. Do not be afraid to lose him. Do not let greed or fear deter you. Collect your money and be happy in the thought that your competitors will thus have the pleasure of doing business with a deadbeat. They probably deserve each other.

Guideline number eight is:

Your small size will limit the amount of credit you can extend to any customer. It will also force you to maintain very light collection procedures.

At the beginning of this chapter I said I did not know how to *get* customers. Instead, I have given some general thoughts on the *nature of customers*. I have done this out of the conviction first, that customers are the reason for being in business, and second, that small businessmen, as a general rule, do not adequately comprehend the degree to which their customers will control their businesses.

Marketing programs are different for different industries. Often, existing patterns of marketing will determine the confines of any conceivable program for getting sales. And since I hope that this book will be read by small businessmen in many different fields, I therefore do not believe it possible to make any specific comments on specialized marketing techniques.

There are a few observations, however, which have been made over the years, and they may prove helpful.

Guideline number two concerned the small company's disability to engage with products that require heavy marketing expense. Such expenses as advertising, for example, must be kept to the barest minimum because the small business just does not have the volume to spread out over advertising costs.

However, a small company does have some real advantages over larger competition. One of the very best of these is its "image."

The small business is usually represented in its sales by the president or a sales manager. The men who do the actual selling, in any case, are very largely also *making the image* of the company. If this is a favorable image, then good. If not, then otherwise.

This "image" is best put forward, in my view, by demonstrating *a demeanor of cautious, yet humble optimism coupled with lots of hard work*. The representative of a small business that can convey this impression has laid the foundation for a great selling success.

Here is the reason why. The small businessman should be humble. He is small, he needs the business, he is asking for the order. It is proper that he should be humble because those are the circumstances. Humility is an endearing quality and gives the ring of credibility to the other parts of the image.

The overall "image" is the small businessman's best tool. (I assume, of course, that his product or service is the equal of his competitors' and that his price is a fair one.) With the "image" thus conveyed, the small businessman has used the

How to Get Customers

one selling tool that will never be available to his large competitors.

Remember, as a small businessman, you can make someone believe he will get extra service and attention on his order simply because your organization is small.

Guideline number nine is:

Your small size should be played up—and properly played up—when calling on your customers. Be humble about it, show cautious optimisim and the willingness to work.

Another observation concerns sales objectives. It is a common complaint with small businessmen that *they never get that really big order.*

Actually, it's probably better that they do not. It would likely throw the whole operation out of balance. This inevitably results somewhere along the line as trouble for the small business and therefore trouble for the customer. In fact, it is very likely the purchasing agent for the customer who knows from experience that this is best, and therefore refuses to give the order.

Small businesses must be satisfied with small orders. Instead of going to the customer looking to take on a big piece of business, the small company should show much more modest aspirations. The orders thus taken can be adequately handled in the smaller size organization and are consistent with the "image," particularly the "cautious" and "humble" parts of it.

It is axiomatic in selling that one should always get the potential buyer to agree with the first several statements. The converse of this is true; avoid a turn-down like the plague because a pattern of disappointment will result.

For the small businessman the object lesson should be clear. By trying for a large order, he runs the risk of being declined on several counts. The solicitation of a small piece of business will more likely result in some business being written—a pattern of success that can be built upon in future selling forays to that account.

How to Get Customers

Guideline number ten is:

Your small size is not adaptive to a large undertaking. Therefore, be satisfied with smaller orders which you can handle and which you have a much better chance of getting.

A third observation is to the point of the number of customers on the active list of a small business. It is so typical that a small businessman will get a good customer, build up a good volume with him and then spend his time servicing that account to the exclusion of getting out and punching new doorbells. It is natural that this happens because it is just a lot easier to deal with one or two customers than with many, and small businessmen are just as human as anyone else.

However, the risks are incalculable. In the chapter on finance, I have already told the case of the industrial equipment manufacturer who had only one type of customer. That was bad enough, and resulted in the business being merged into a larger company. When the cosmetics and toilet articles manufacturer found his one big customer was broke and could not or would not pay, the loss forced him into bankruptcy because, in addition to the loss, he had no other large customers to keep him going. The results were just as unhappy in another situation.

We had financed a manufacturer of a leisure-time product. This operation had been growing profitably for some five years. Our financing was for the purpose of lowering interest costs on borrowed funds and recasting some short-term debt into longer-term securities. All went well the first year.

This was a seasonal business and there were nearly six months of the year when there were virtually no sales. It seemed to make sense to at least try to develop another business which would have a busy season corresponding to the slow season of the existing business.

Such a business was found and on the first year of operations, beginning with no sales backlogs and no product history or acceptance, nearly $200,000 of goods were sold. It was very encouraging. The next year, with a backlog of orders of $200,000, sales were a little over $400,000. The third year, the opening backlog was nearly $800,000. The company geared up to do a million dollars in sales based on past experience. Actual sales were $1.2 million. It appeared that a profitable item had been established and management congratulated itself on having made a wise decision.

But the selling pattern that had developed over this period had caused some difficulties. There were many smaller accounts that required a heavy burden of servicing time and were not particularly prompt in the payment of their bills. There were also several larger accounts, and these were characterized by the small amount of servicing and the more prompt payment of their invoices. The decision was therefore made to concentrate on the several large accounts in the coming year.

The backlog at the beginning of the fourth year was nearly $1.5 million. Ninety per cent of the backlog was to four of the larger customers from the previous years. Management programmed sales of $2 million based on past experience. That year there was a glut on the market of similar products and actual shipments were less than $800,000.

This resulted in the company's having a severe cash problem for the season of their regular established business because of having all that cash tied up in an inventory of products which would not be saleable until the following year, if at all. Somehow, in spite of this cash bind, the company managed to get through its regular season.

It had been decided that the next season for the new item would be based solely on selling the inventory on hand carried over from the past season. But such was not to work out.

The four larger customers themselves had been left with heavy inventories from the previous season and the re-orders received totalled less than $200,000. At the end of the fifth season, there remained nearly ¾ million dollars' worth of unsold merchandise. This inventory was now two years old and represented at best a loss of 80 per cent of its value even if it could have been liquidated—which it could not.

To make a quick end to a sad tale, this history resulted in the company's going bankrupt.

The point of the story here is to illustrate the danger of relying on a few customers who account for the largest percentage of a company's volume. To be sure, in the case described there were other important considerations that forced the company into bankruptcy. However, one of the most significant of these considerations was its inability to move the inventory. This inability was aggravated by the few accounts the company had and the ill-will it had created with the many smaller accounts. This latter circumstance was brought about when the company refused to write anything but large orders and effectively eliminated this group of customers as a possible source of sales.

Guideline number 11 is:

Your small size makes you very vulnerable to a sales decline. This vulnerability is greatly expanded if a significant portion of your sales are to a few customers. It is greatly reduced if the majority of your sales are to a high number of small accounts.

Some small businessmen become involved in what I consider to be the most stupid of all possible activities—selling below cost. They may do this for several reasons, among which I have already mentioned general price declines which force them down with everyone else. But sometimes they sell below cost because they do not know what price to charge.

This ridiculous situation usually develops from one of two reasons; either they do not know their costs or they do not know how to get the price they need to make a profit. When I encounter this situation I am always tempted to close the proceedings right then and there.

How to Get Customers

Why? Because a man who is sufficiently naïve to sell below cost is "living with the brownies," as they say. If he does not know his costs, he is a fool. If he knows his costs and recognizes that he is selling below cost, then he is giving his business away to his customers, and he is also a fool. Yet, as I mentioned in the case of the manufacturer of electrical contractors' supplies, it is sometimes done, and in that case I was a party to the decision. It never works out, and I should have known it.

Take the situation where the small business has just a few customers out of many that will not pay a price that will produce a profit. This situation is most frequently found where the small business has one, two or a few large customers. The theory is that if the small business were to lose any of its accounts, the volume thus lost would make the remaining volume unprofitable.

This theory is fallacious for the reason that sales which do not produce adequate profits because of low price structures to large customers tend to erode the small business over a long period of time. The fact that the profits are inadequate means nothing more or less than that the company is gradually *giving* its capital to the customers in the same amount by which profits are inadequate. Moreover, when the volume which would be lost if the few large customers were lost is sufficient to make the remaining volume unprofitable in spite of the better prices being obtained, then the small businessman is doubly damned.

In other words, if your product is priced in such a way that any but the smallest percentage is sold at inadequate rates, then the product is not adequately priced for *all* customers. If one or two customers refuse to pay a sufficient price, it is the same as if all customers for that product were refusing to pay a sufficient price. Think of it this way: Suppose there are 50 customers for your product, of whom five account for half the sales and the remaining 45 the other half; prices to the five large accounts are lower than to the 45 smaller accounts; prices to the five are of a level that do not return an adequate profit, but sales are made because of the "volume" which, it is believed, lowers the costs on the sales to the remaining 45 accounts at higher prices. Now suppose the small business operator could replace the five large accounts with a new group at 45 smaller accounts so that no volume were lost. Would he, in that case, offer this new group—*as a group*—the same lower prices? Almost certainly not, I think.

Although I have no figures of my own to substantiate it, I venture the guess that at least half the small business failures have, as one ingredient, the fact that the product or service is sold below cost. For this reason I state confidently that the ability to price correctly the product or service is as important as any other single aspect of the small businessman's job.

What about price? Without meaning to sound dogmatic about it, let's set the record straight; price is almost always the only consideration in making a sale. What is forgotten by so many small businessmen is what goes into setting the price, what things go into making the price acceptable.

Earlier I spoke about pricing in terms of the great advantage in having a product that can be sold on the basis of value to the customer, savings he might make by using the product or service. Not every small business is lucky enough to have products like that or is able to build such features into his product or service.

Sometimes, a small businessman finds himself in the unenviable positions of having a product or service that he simply cannot price high enough to make a profit. In spite of all his cost cutting, all the extra services he can afford to provide, all the efforts he can make, the price he can get still is not enough. For such a small businessman, the best thing he can do is get out of that line at the soonest possible date.

Guideline number 12 is:

You must know your costs accurately in order to set prices.

How to Get Customers

There are circumstances when it is impossible to get an adequate price. Be smart and get out as quickly as possible. As a small businessman you cannot afford customers who will not pay an adequate price and you cannot afford a product line you are forced, by whatever reason, to sell at a loss.

It will probably be impossible for any small business to cover all the guidelines in its relationships with its customers. In that case, the guidelines are recommended as points to look out for in the sales programs of any small business.

There is no question whatever, in my mind, that the successful implementation of the small business's marketing program will be the single most important ingredient in its growth. *Your customers will make your business.*

Each industry, each type of small business, from a small corner delivery market to a dry cleaning establishment, to a manufacturers' representative organization, to an engineering consulting firm, to a manufacturer of anything from bobby pins to air conditioners—each will have its own method of getting its customers.

Perhaps customers will be obtained by direct mail on a national coverage basis, or by ringing doorbells in a single neighborhood, or by advertising in trade journals, or by having salesmen call direct, or through jobbers and representatives. Whatever the method, that which best suits a given small business is the method to use.

In each case the selection of the method or methods will be important. But equally important will be the manner in which the small business operator sets up his company's relationships with its customers.

That is what the guidelines are for. They will provide a useful way of thinking about the problems of being small.

4

How to Select Products

The reader will by now have begun to get the impression that being small means that a business will have restraints and confines placed upon it. That is, he will have gotten this impression if I have done my job correctly. In any event, the impression is accurate.

In the discussions about financing your small business and about the types of customers you might find most appropriate in terms of the limitations placed on you by your size, we have talked about two aspects of your business in which it is a necessary concomitant of success that you convince someone outside your direct control to act in a certain way.

In selecting products, that circumstance is changed. In this area, the small businessman has the actions under his own control. His decision-making in this area, however, will dictate a large measure of any problems he may have later on with his banks and his customers.

One other consideration is necessary before discussing the products which are appropriate to small business. That is the close affinity existing between the nature of the products and services of a small business and its customers. It is not possible to discuss one without the other, for both the product and the customer are inevitably involved in the need-satisfaction relationship.

How to Select Products

Therefore, a good portion of this chapter will deal with matters already covered from another point of view in the preceding chapter. And since the means of making the product or providing the service must be purchased or otherwise acquired, the discussion about products will also include reference to the discussion of finance.

Every now and then someone comes into my office with a proposal that is very interesting, and may even be feasible, but does not lend itself to the confines of a small business. On occasion it is all one can do to keep from laughing in the man's face.

The other day I received a call asking for an appointment. At these times, it is normal to ask for some information about the proposal the caller has in mind to present. Not infrequently it is possible to learn enough about the deal to tell the man that it sounds interesting or that it doesn't. The caller may refuse to give any information, saying that he can only do justice to his proposal in a face-to-face conference.

I was, therefore, forewarned when the caller made that statement to my inquiry. Experience with such men has led me to the conclusion that the proposal will have something unusual connected with it. And this man's proposal was unusual.

He proposed to air-condition the city of Los Angeles.

On another day, a man walked into our offices and asked to see "the boss." Apparently he would not settle for anyone else and after one of my associates had been rebuffed, he was shown into my room. The first thing he did was to look quite closely all around the room for any microphones or other so-called "bugging" devices. Then, after asking that my associate leave the room, he closed the door.

The best way I can describe this man is that he reminded me of nothing so much as the characters that played the anarchists in the old movies, the ones who wore beards, long black coats and carried little black bombs under their arms. He had a furtive look and acted very nervous.

How to Select Products

Then he got into his pitch. As he began to talk his nervousness seemed to increase and his eyes grew bright and large. His story was tragic, the way he told it, a tale of one disaster after another, sickness, heartache and death. Failure had followed failure. This part of his story took nearly 15 minutes to tell.

He then continued his story by relating how his troubles all began in the first place. It had to do with his invention, the one he wanted my company to finance. This invention had so incensed this man's gods that they, in their turn, had brought woe and misery on him and his whole house.

The man had invented special shoes that would enable him to walk on water.

Both the proposals had several aspects in common. In each case, the men were completely and absolutely convinced of the need for their proposals. As to air-conditioning Los Angeles, there is no one who could gainsay the good effects of such a proposal. The ability to walk on water would be helpful in many circumstances. My own view is that both proposals are not practical as ventures for small business. The funds required for the Los Angeles project were more than $25 million. The other man asked for $500 to make a few samples of his buoyant shoes.

Let me dispel the impression, if it exists, that I wish or intend to poke fun at either of these men. After all, it is my job to listen to every proposal and try to decide if it is the germ of an idea or project that could be profitable for a small business. I am always reminded of a friend of mine who pointed out to me one day that if I did not know such a thing as radio existed I would say it was impossible. He is correct, of course. I live in the hopes that one day someone will walk into my office with a project that will have the same potential as the radio. To serve this hope I will talk with anyone, any time, at any place.

To return to the two proposals, it was my view that neither of them contained the ingredients necessary to build a business. With the Los Angeles project, the need for funds of such magnitude immediately disqualified it from further consideration. It is worth mentioning, however, that the proposal made good sense and, on paper at least, provided a means of accomplishing the objective, as vast as it is. There was nothing in the man's program which was unique, unproven or unpractical. The cost to the city of Los Angeles was even reasonable, and came out to something under 15 cents per day per individual.

As to the shoes that would enable a man to walk on water, I doubt that a business could be built with them as the product. I have no idea how such shoes would be sold, but I believe the proposal of the inventor to sell them through church groups would not be workable. In any case, the shoes could not be made by any established process. According to the inventor, these shoes could only be made by people who "believed" (his word) the shoes would work. I cannot remember now if such "believing" was also required on the part of the wearer.

Admittedly these two cases are extremes. It is one of the interesting aspects of my business that these types of things come up from time to time. For the most part, however, the product a man is making or contemplates making—or a service if that is his "product"—falls into several reasonable catagories. And since the selection of product or service is largely the decision of the small businessman himself, this is an area of choice that deserves the closest possible attention.

I believe that most small businesses get started because of an idea about a product—a better way to make it or a better way to sell it.

Take the case of a company with which I am completely familiar. This illustrates very well the development of a small business from an idea to an established concern. The business was formed by two young men who had an idea of a better way to make a standard industrial product. Over the

How to Select Products

years since then they have branched out into related fields, but always with the same basic idea as to their product.

The product they selected was characterized by several important facts:

1. It was essential in the finishing of certain other products.

2. These other products were made almost exclusively by very large, well-established manufacturing concerns.

3. The "work" the company was to do involved the design of and machining work on large pieces of various materials, mostly metal; the company was to supply the former, the customer the latter.

4. A good deal of service was involved and the essence of the continuing business was the repeat aspect.

5. The amount of work that each large customer required was not enough to warrant his going into the field himself.

6. The actual machining work required very skilled craftsmen.

This is a near perfect score on the selection of a product for a small business. Let's take each product characteristic again and analyze it in detail:

1. It was essential. This is a good beginning. It has long been my own view that *no small business should get started on a product that is not essential.* So many of the small business failures I have seen are the results of a basic failure on this point. It is agreed that the "essentiality" relates to the customer, but remember that we are here describing the product or service in terms of its characteristics. The characteristic of "essentiality" thus is applied to the product while it derives from the customer.

When a small business is formed with a product that has this quality or characteristic, it has begun its life on a firm foundation. As far as the customer is concerned, he must buy the product or service from someone. I have always taken exception to the old saying about the world beating a path to

How to Select Products

the door of the man who builds a better mousetrap. We already have acceptable mousetraps, in the United States at any rate, and I don't believe a man could sell any significant amount of a better mousetrap.

Guideline number 1 is:

If at all possible, select a product or service that is essential to your customers.

2. The product was used in the processes of large, well-established concerns. This consideration is especially applicable to a small manufacturing concern, although it may not apply so directly to service organizations. For the small manufacturing company, it means that the ultimate consumer, as distinguished from the company's customer, is being catered to by large, well-established, well-financed organizations. This means the small company is relying on the large company to create, maintain and sell the ultimate, broad consumer market, a task probably well beyond the capabilities of the small supplier.

Guideline number 2 is:

It is particularly appropriate for a small company to provide products or services which become part of something larger.

3. The product was actually the design of and machine work on materials owned by the large companies. How perfect!

It is not always possible to contrive such circumstances. Indeed they are very rare in my experience. Usually the manufacturing concern is required to purchase the raw materials and component parts, do his work on them, and sell them. Frequently, the ultimate selling price of the product has very little relation to the work performed or the value added in manufacture or assembly.

In the service industry a similar circumstance is found in a dry cleaning establishment. The company supplies the cleansers and the pressers. *The customer supplies the suit.* This characteristic, albeit rare, is nonetheless very worthy of

How to Select Products

attention. One of the chronic complaints of small business is that the products or services they provide cost so much to make that they are continually strapped for working capital.

But the point is this. In the company I am discussing the only sales were those showing *value added*. Since they were not required to own the large metal pieces, their sales truly reflected the work they had performed. When a small businessman tells you of his sales, be sure to inquire as to the ingredients of his product. The real test of profitability is the profit on the work done by the company, not on the ultimate selling price.

Guideline number 3 is:

Your manufacturing or process operation exists only to add value to the materials required. In selecting your product or service try to pick a line where there is the least possible cost to your company for the required materials.

4. The product was characterized by heavy service requirements and a repetition of the work performed. These are two qualities that are especially attractive to small businesses.

The service aspect connected with a product is one of the strongest possible incentives to a small businessman. Products which require special service lend themselves very well to the abilities of a small organization. This group should be able to move quickly and its small size lends itself to personalized service—a more intimate involvement on the part of the personnel concerned.

Usually, when service is an ingredient or characteristic of the product, there will also be a repeat nature to the business. This is perfectly logical. A customer who requires service with his purchases will naturally return to the small seller for future business in order to maintain and enhance, if possible, the service aspect (provided the product and service are good, of course).

From the small businessman's point of view, the service he gives also means he is keeping close tabs on his customer

How to Select Products

because of a characteristic of his product. This relationship, properly and competently nurtured, will result in the repeat business that is always so profitable. One word of caution is necessary, however. Because the customer-supplier relationship is so strong, it will be all the more difficult to get business away from the competition. Your ability to get new business in a situation like this will probably be in direct proportion to the degree of the customer's dissatisfaction with his present supplier. In any case, guideline number 4 is:

Your small size will enable you to give much attention to any servicing that attends your product or service. Try to pick products or lines that have these characteristics because they usually lead to a close relationship with the customer and mean repeat business.

5. The volume for any one customer was sufficiently small that it was not economical for the customer to make the product himself. The customer could buy cheaper than he could make.

There is always the disadvantage to a small company that it will lose its customers for no other reason than that the customer can save money or accomplish some other desirable objective by doing the job himself.

I was once a director of a company that manufactured a line of leisure-time products for the family. We sold certain of the items through distributors who were local businessmen in their communities. The product is such that two or three unskilled workers can be trained to make all of it except one essential part that requires considerable heavy machinery.

The man who was running the business was continually reporting to his board that a distributor had gone into business for himself. This always infuriated the manager so that for several days after learning of it his ulcer would put him in bed.

Yet, try as we did, the directors could never get the manager to understand that the development of a distributor to a point where he was able to go into business himself

How to Select Products

represented the best of all possible circumstances. The distributor had grown to a successful size through the company's efforts, which meant that they both had made money. To lose him at that point was unfortunate, but should not have been the cause of such misery.

In this case, it was a quality of the product that at a certain point the simple manufacturing process, the unskilled labor required, and the ready availability of the new materials in small amounts led to the expected loss of a customer who had prospered.

There are times, however, when the product will not be so characterized. The same type of situation will frequently occur when the volume of a product reaches a level where economies obtained in large runs will make it possible for the customer to make cheaper than he can buy. In the case of the company we were discussing, the volume of machining the highly specialized equipment required to accomplish it and the orientation of the customers toward putting their efforts in the products they were processing with this equipment all added up to a product quality that is much to be desired.

Guideline number 5 is: *An advantage of being small is that production runs can be shorter but still profitable as compared to the longer runs required for profitable operations in large companies. Try to select as your product or service one that has this quality. It is one product quality that derives directly from your small size.*

6. There was a large degree of know-how. This ingredient is practically indispensable if a product is to become established and permanent. It is the one ingredient that distinguishes a product from its imitators, and the proper know-how properly applied can be the best possible insurance against product instability.

During the early 1950's I was one of a group of young men who undertook to show foreign businessmen around selected industries in this country. The Japanese and the Ger-

How to Select Products

mans were the most inquisitive and asked the most questions.

But the Germans in particular seemed never to be satisfied. They wanted to keep going into more and more detail, and they seemed to be looking for something they could never find. At dinner one night, I asked one of the men just what it was they were trying to find out. The answer took most of the evening to tell, but in summary they were looking for the "leader" who was responsible in each plant for the productivity.

Apparently, the Germans thought there was a man in each factory who was the genius behind the high rate of production, a man who was responsible for product design, another for engineering, etc. And over all these geniuses was the "super-genius," the man who knew all and could accomplish all.

The reply to the Germans answer is in those two words, "know-how." We have come to hyphenate the word, and it is, I believe, as good a word as there is to describe the collective genius of our country to make things. The Germans may have thought of it as coming from one man, but actually it was just good old Yankee ingenuity at work on a large and collective basis.

Since then I have often wondered if the marvelous productivity the West Germans have shown could in any way be ascribed to the realization that "know-how" is a way of making a good product.

Know-how is often a small company's claim to a rightful existence. I worked for several years for a small company in Cleveland that based its major product lines on know-how. It was in an industry that dealt with complicated chemical formulas and processes. The product itself required skill and training to use properly.

We sustained a fire that destroyed that part of our plant which made the applications of the chemical formulas which were most closely guarded as company secrets. In order to

How to Select Products

supply our customers during the period when we were rebuilding, we were forced to tell another company how we made our formulas and applied them, with the understanding that when we were once again able to manufacture the products ourselves they would not compete against us!

To return to the example company, in its case the know-how was the product of designers and engravers who translated their work into very precise machining operations. There was craft and skill at every step of the way. Again, it was a substantial contribution to the stability of their product line.

Guideline number 6 is: *Your small size will limit your production ability where quantity is concerned. It will in no way limit your ability to bring know-how to your manufacturing operations and will thereby permit you to introduce, by this means alone, an important aspect of exclusivity to your product or service.*

Earlier I discussed the small business that was built on the idea of acquiring small stamping houses for the purpose of building up an inventory of tooling to be used in the lighting-fixture trade. Among the interesting side benefits of this program has been what it has done for the company in terms of competitors. This is by no means a large company, yet it is very nearly competition-proof because even the largest companies would not find it profitable to invest in the tooling required to compete.

This company has built its business on the basis of the equipment needed to make its products, an excellent basis for a small business. And again, the plan lent itself to the peculiarities of small size. To another small company, the inventory cost of tooling is staggering; to a large company it would be a bother in terms of the ultimate volume that might be obtained. In either case, a good deal of competition has been pre-empted.

Guideline number 7 is: *Your small size will limit you in the amount you can invest in production equipment. If you*

How to Select Products

can make your investment in tooling or equipment and in so doing gain a measure of exclusivity, your small size will not be the competitive hindrance it might be otherwise.

Another company with which I am familiar has achieved something of a similar position, but by different means. It is a leather tannery.

In the tanning business, I am told, there is really no way to tell when hides are ready to be withdrawn from the tanning baths and dried except by a person who "knows" when they are. Apprenticeships in a tannery even today run an average of five years.

Drying the hides is equally important and again it takes a man walking through the great drying racks and frames to "feel" the hides, the heat of the air and its moisture, to know how long to continue the drying process and to regulate the machinery during the period.

The tannery of which I speak has developed a means of tanning hides from water buffaloes, an accomplishment not presently duplicated, I am told. The leather is excellent for children's shoes.

But while the company does not anticipate sales of these hides to contribute a substantial volume, the ability to make such hides and have them available for sale has greatly helped the company in the sales of its other products. The tanning trade has been practiced for centuries. It is still based on the special ability of a tanner to get the desired results from his hides. The ability to deliver such quality consistently has resulted in product stability for this company's entire line.

Tanneries can run into large capital investments, a drawback to being small. But this company, by the development of one item of exclusivity, has overcome the disadvantage of competing with larger concerns in the field. It has achieved a generally stable product-acceptance where only one product out of several dozen is unique.

Guideline number 8 is: *Your larger competitors will have*

How to Select Products

more capital invested and probably a much broader product line. Your small company may well be able to compete effectively if only one of your items has the important aspect of exclusivity, and lends this to your entire line.

There was some publicity recently about American Motors which indicated it had been classified as a small business for purposes of being awarded government contracts. American Motors, with sales of more than $900 million, could only be considered small by comparison with General Motors and Ford.

There is something to being smaller than your competitors, though, particularly when it comes to making your product. This is because there are economic sizes to things and there are certain processes which would not lend themselves to large production even if the capital were available to invest.

A good example is a small company we were going to finance but then decided not to. We didn't because the owners came up with the money themselves. It was a nice business, though, and otherwise we would have arranged a long-term loan.

They harvested various crops of seafood and then processed, packed and sold them under their own label through normal food jobbers and distributors. They came to us for money because they had stumbled on a way of cleaning certain of the seafood items that was unique and worked very well. It involved spending a sum for equipment which was perfectly reasonable for a small business.

During my investigation I asked about the competition from the much larger companies in the same field, and what was to prevent them from doing the same thing only on a much larger scale. The managers of our prospective client pointed out to me that it would not be possible to build such equipment any larger than they proposed and, after I had studied their analysis, I had to agree. They reasoned that their present small size would allow them a long period of

How to Select Products

exclusivity to the process and that they would never face competition from the large concerns.

With the money we would have advanced, but which they finally put up themselves, they built their equipment. There was nothing patentable or secret about it, so very shortly the large companies were trying to adapt the process to their operations. They were not successful.

Guideline number 9 is: *Your small size will make certain types of operations profitable to you while your larger competitors, because of their size, will be unable to adopt your methods. This is an excellent way for a small business to gain exclusivity for its product.*

A footnote to the foregoing story might be interesting. The owners of the seafood business are pleased with the improved quality of their product, thanks to the processing innovation. They have been able to raise prices and improve and up-grade their distribution. They are also aware they cannot grow in size, but their increased profits tend to make them willing to accept this inconvenience. As the saying goes, "they are crying all the way to the bank."

In the discussion of customers, I introduced the thought that there was a useful way of thinking about them, and that was to put them in a "time span" chart and plot the length of time *in the future* that the customers had to be lined up and the production of your small company sold or, at the least, marketed in the sense of having your customer contacts made and channels of distribution established.

The point was made that, according to the type of product you were making in your small business, your marketing decisions would have to be made in various time-spans. The same time-span is also involved in decision-making when it comes to planning your production facilities.

It is very commonplace nowadays to have a "facilities brochure." These booklets or reports are prepared by the company for the purpose of showing potential customers the type of work the company can do. Many small companies I

How to Select Products

know of have these reports. By and large they tend to overstate what the company can do, and I have seen only one such report from a small business that put the emphasis where it belonged—on the company's ability to provide a production facility staffed with a management that put its decision-making into the time-span context.

The "facilities review" is also commonplace. It is part of the same general emphasis that has spawned the facilities brochure. In such a review, a team of specialists comes from the customer and takes a tour of the plant. They examine the production equipment, inventory controls, shipping and reviewing departments, purchasing department, engineering, quality control, etc.

I suppose it is a basically sound idea, and it probably weeds out a lot of second-rate companies. But in small business it is usually a joke. Most small businesses have one and possibly three or four men who are in charge of everything. It is one of the disadvantages of being small that each member of management must wear a number of hats.

In the one case I mentioned where the facilities brochure emphasized the time-span of decision-making factor, the point was made that the company *would not take on* any business that required more than *three months' lead-time.* That is, a potential customer was advised that if his project would require more than three months to engineer, to obtain machinery, to purchase the required materials or anything else connected with the work before shipments were commenced, the company would decline the work.

The results of this statement have been very beneficial to the company. It has implemented a policy of limiting itself to jobs that fit this time-span. The mere making of the statement lends much credibility to the entire facilities brochure. They have said, in effect, the limit of their resources can be expressed in terms of the time they can spend on any one project to get it started, and they have stated what that time limit is. By the way, this is the same small business I have

How to Select Products

mentioned several times before as having done a very good job—the one formed by the engineer and the accountant.

Guideline number 10 is: *Your small size will place limits on every aspect of your ability to acquire productive assets. This is nowhere more apparent than when it comes to time. Small companies almost without exception should select products which do not require heavy amounts of this precious commodity.*

It has been my experience that most small businesses get started full-blown. That is, the day they are formed, the management or owners already know what their product will be. I have never heard of a business getting started on the basis that after it was formed it would undertake to develop a product or service.

The reason for this is simple. To form a business other than to undertake whatever project it has at hand would be to form it prematurely. But the point is this: Time has already been spent in the development of the product or service, at least an idea of the customers has already been formed, and distribution has been planned. In short, the founders of the small business have already made the *investment of time.*

It is a pity they are not so careful when they take their next move!

An excellent example of what happens when they are not careful was to be seen in the demise of the small appliance manufacturer I mentioned earlier while discussing finance. I do not recall now how long the company had been going with its line of appliances before they purchased the additional business, but it was in excess of six years. The decision to expand was made overnight!

The longer span required in the manufacturing cycle of the newly acquired business went completely unnoticed in the planning. The assumption was that since so many of the business aspects of the new lines were similar to the existing lines, there would be no problems assimilating the new; just

How to Select Products

adding it on would be all that was required. As I pointed out, the longer time-span involved with the inventory began working against the company within 90 days.

In certain types of businesses, the inventory has qualities inherent in itself that will create the need for decision-making in a time-span. For example, I once financed a vintner. In this company, inventories must be held for a certain period in order to age. In another company, the product is lumber, and this too must be allowed to "cure" before being kiln dried and manufactured into flooring. Still another company has fresh garden produce which must be marketed immediately.

In each of the companies above, there are also special methods of handling the inventory. The vintner must have large, specially made casks and a cool, dark room to store them in. Someone must tend them and test the wine. The tester is an artisan who has had not less than a 10-year apprenticeship. The lumber the flooring manufacturer buys must be stored in an open yard with spacing sticks between each layer of boards. The lumber must be turned and inspected and tended for 90 to 120 days. The farm that grows the fresh produce can store part of its crop in huge refrigerated buildings, and the trucks or railway cars that transport it must be refrigerated.

The manufacturer of chemicals I mentioned in discussing customers had an inventory problem of still different complexion. When the company had completed its manufacturing plant and found it "on stream," sufficient customers had not been obtained to take the production. This company's problem was that beyond a certain very small amount, the chemicals were impossible to store. The entire plant had to be shut down because it could only make the amount of chemicals it was designed to make at one time.

Guideline number 11 is: *Inventory problems will vary according to the type of inventory, what it is made of, its perishability or special storage and handling requirements,*

How to Select Products

and the manufacturing techniques and processes by which it is created. Your small size will limit your flexibility in dealing with such problems.

The way a product is made can sometimes be its strongest quality. There was a time when I kept a tally sheet on which I marked down those businesses I learned about that were formed because someone had an idea of how to make something in a better or more economical way than existed at the time. After a period of six months I gave it up for the simple reason that the sample I obtained had confirmed my guess—about 85 per cent of the small manufacturing companies that are formed are the result of the founders' thinking that they had a better way of making the product. The other 15 per cent were those who thought they could sell their product better.

Only infrequently is their assumption correct. Usually, such men have not made a sufficiently thorough examination of the situation. But once in a while, their program is successful.

One such success involved a man who was a specialist in design, especially of packaging machinery. His experience had been with several major companies where his work had earned him a good reputation. Then one day he was sent by his employer to visit a customer who had a packaging problem.

This customer manufactured home toilet accessories, nursery items and medical supplies. One of their products was made on machines that were quite complicated and which made large quantities of one of their items each day. The man apparently took one look at the machines and immediately saw a better way to make the machine. He spent the next 18 months working nights in his basement building the prototype of his machine. Eventually, he had a design that worked.

His machine had certain very distinct advantages over those in use. It would make 50 per cent more of the product

How to Select Products

in the same time. It required two skilled operators and one helper to run compared with six skilled operators and a helper needed for the old machine; the quality was improved and was subject to checking while the machine was still running, whereas the older machine had to be shut off. The new machine cost more to build, but not significantly more.

The man has been able to raise the funds required to build ten of the machines and has arranged for the sale of his output through some private deals by which he will manufacture for companies under their brand names. They will, in turn, market the products through their established organization.

This man has been able to start a business on the basis of cost. Because his machines can manufacture a product that is competitive in quality at a price that is lower than what can be done with previously existing machinery, the man can sell on the basis of price. His machines have several features on which patents have been solicited to give him some protection for a few years.

Although this small business has not yet completed its first year of operations, it is my guess that the company will make the grade. This estimate is based on the demonstrated ability of the new machines to do what they are supposed to do. The inventor had spent the time to prove his idea before he started his business.

On the other hand, a company I know of has spent over three million dollars trying to get a process to work. This process was a way of making color TV tubes of an improved quality. The technique of getting the image on the screen was the key to this process. The inventor had made a few handmade samples. These he showed to prospective investors. The performance of these tubes was clearly far superior to what is on the market today. I have seen the tubes myself and they are very good.

The trouble developed in trying to get a commercially

How to Select Products

economical method of making them. The handmade samples were much too expensive for any kind of sales program. Many different techniques were tried. All ended in failure. There is one crucial process in laying down some sort of screen that just does not lend itself to any known mass-production methods. All the investors' money has been wasted and to date there has not been any progress toward solving the manufacturing problems.

I have always enjoyed tinkering with engines. I keep a collection of malfunctioning motors in my workshop just to have something to fix, and I believe I must have a dozen or more motors that run perfectly but for which I have no use other than to run them and thereby give myself pleasure.

Imagine my delight, then, when one day a man came in who claimed to have developed a lightweight, air-cooled diesel engine. One would have to know something about the problems associated with diesel engines to understand the great advantages inherent in a small horsepower, lightweight diesel engine. There are some important advantages to this type of power unit, and if they were ever available, I believe they would have a very wide sale.

In the present case, however, there has never been any production of the engines. Our investigation of the proposal indicated the designer had several working models. These he had made over a period of a year at a time three years before he had come to see us. The obvious question was, why had he stopped there? Why had he not made some more engines for testing purposes? Why had he been unable to obtain some actual field experience, even if he had been required to give an engine to some potential user?

The answer was not immediately available, but a little digging into the man's background and a detailed history of his work on the engine indicated the man could never phase out a design. That is to say, he would never get to a point in the development of anything where he would stop further

[100]

How to Select Products

development, adopt his design as standard, and get down to the business of making some engines.

Rather, he would continuously work at further design and development. As he worked on one aspect of the engine, ideas would occur to him as to how to improve some other feature. Then, while working on this feature, someone would suggest a new application and he would undertake to design an entirely new engine for that use. We declined the proposal to finance this operation, but we did tell the man that when he had standardized his engine, when he had phased out its development and was ready to get into production, we would then reconsider the matter. That was three years ago and I believe he is still tinkering.

Guideline number 12 is: *You do not have a product until you are in a position to make it consistently, of a quality and at a cost that is acceptable to the customer. Particularly in a small business, with limited resources, it is essential that this point be reached quickly. Your small size will not be a hindrance if through the production methods, special designs and the like you can secure a proprietary interest in the method of manufacture.*

In setting up your small plant, service facility or what have you, there is currently in vogue in this country a wide range of franchises. These run all the way from franchises to re-manufacture transmissions on automobiles to running roadside hamburger palaces. The franchise operator is assisted by the franchiser and there is usually a geographical exclusivity to the franchise as well as product exclusivity.

Franchising is by no means new. Most soft drink bottling operations have been operated under franchises since the beginning of the soda-pop industry. I would class automobile dealerships in the same general category. Manufacturers' representatives operate in the same way. This type of set-up is where the local businessman makes a contract with the parent company under which the parent supplies him with

How to Select Products

products, equipment and training and he supplies the capital, labor force and local sales efforts. It is an excellent means of establishing a small business.

The small businessman who makes a contract with such a franchising parent company is buying experience and proven product. Usually there is also much information on sales and marketing techniques and costs. In most cases, the small businesses thus formed are not subject to the risks of unproven product, unproven manufacturing processes, unproven selling techniques. These items, having been demonstrated and proven, are what the small businessman is paying for when he buys the franchise. I do not believe it is possible to learn the equivalent lessons, gain the equivalent experience and otherwise obtain the background of knowledge about a business at anywhere near the cost of most franchises. It is the cheapest money a man can spend.

In most cases, the franchise operator obtains production or manufacturing know-how. The roadside hamburger stands that operate under national franchises are programmed to the finest detail. The operator gets the most accurate and detailed set of instructions I have ever seen. Most of the problems usually associated with a small business have been anticipated, including inventory controls, purchasing activities, personnel selection and training, and on and on.

Parenthetically, some of these operators fail in business in spite of all the knowledge available to them. I have not seen a study of the failures in such franchising operations, but one should be made. It is my guess that such a study would show that such failures derive from two sources: the carelessness of the operator or the unsuitability of the location of the franchise.

But franchising is not the only way to obtain such knowledge, and there is a disadvantage to having such knowledge made so readily available. Knowledge is one thing; the experience and ability to implement the knowledge is another. The easy availability of knowledge and its accumulation are

How to Select Products

sometimes confused with the ability to effectually apply the knowledge.

In any case, Guideline number 13 is: *It is frequently possible to start your small business with a well-developed background of knowledge and experience, particularly in the areas of manufacturing or production. One way of obtaining such information is through franchising. Try to select your product from among those that have such knowledge available or acquire it for the products you already have.*

I have a pet phrase to describe the man who has a lot of knowledge but is incapable of making it useful. I call him a "dumb genius." The woods are full of his type.

One such man's company was involved in the electronics field. He manufactured a line of products which were part of a much larger complex of parts which themselves were then brought together to make the final product. He was in the same position as the man who makes wheels of different sizes for automobiles, trucks, buses and railroad cars. His products were part of a much larger number of products that, when assembled together in a certain way, made the automobile.

The man's business went along quite well at the start and some modest profits were made. Then the man was able to raise a large amount of cash from an investment banking firm. His troubles started at that point.

Now he had the financial reserves to build an inventory. He could take on production methods different from the jobshop operation he had been running, and by standardizing on larger production, thereby reduce costs. First, however, he decided to redesign his product line.

At this point, he began to work feverishly on his new designs. He brought all his genius (and he *was* a genius in his field) to bear on the problems of his industry. The product line he developed was quite different from his old line and he ordered production runs to begin. All during this time, he had been working alone. He had not consulted his customers or his own production people. The fact was that

How to Select Products

he did know of a better way to do the job, and that is what he designed.

The only problem that developed was a catastrophe. What this man had done was the same as a wheel maker's designing wheels that would work only if there were something other than rubber tires to put on them. His answer to his customers who would not buy, indeed could not use, his new designs was along the lines of saying that he knew how to make what was required in the place of tires, and he told them what it was. When the customers said they would not change just for the new products he had designed, the man would become furious and end the conversation.

Perhaps, if he had handled the situation differently, the man could have made a great breakthrough in his special technology. He acted, however, as a dumb genius. He did not, and still does not, understand why his business failed with its shelves loaded with a beautifully made inventory of superior parts at a very good price which nobody would buy.

It is typical of small manufacturing companies particularly that they emphasize their ability to "move fast" on product design and innovation. It is proper for them to do so, because it is a characteritic of small business that it can move more rapidly than a larger, more cumbersome organization. However, as in the case described above, moving too quickly can sometimes lead to disaster. After four years, the electronics company is just now seeing the industry catch up to this man's thinking. Perhaps, if other techniques were not now available, his inventory of advanced designed products could be sold. Unfortunately, there are improved materials and techniques today that would obsolete the inventory in any case.

The ability to move rapidly is one of the advantages ascribed to a small business. There is a strong note of caution, however, that should always accompany your thinking about your small business's products or services. There is a very important difference between moving quickly and innovat-

How to Select Products

ing, and I think many small businessmen fail to make this distinction.

There is a case I observed some three years ago that illustrates the manner in which a small business can move quickly and beat its larger competitors.

A company of which I was a director manufactured a part for refrigerators, the part that controls the automatic ice-making device. It is essentially a sensing instrument that can tell when the ice has been made and then activates a motor that empties the ice tray. The company actually got into this business because its engineers could move quickly on a new development. This small business is, again, the company formed by the engineer and the accountant.

This small business had established a relationship with the largest maker of refrigerators, but was not at the time furnishing them with the ice-making device. At the time of a visit to the large company, the small business engineer happened to attend a meeting at which there were described the problems being found with the ice-making device the large company was using at the time. New materials were available and a new technique developed which were thought to hold much promise toward eliminating those problems.

However, in the large company, development work of the nature required would take several months at best. The small businessman said he believed he could move much more rapidly than that if given the opportunity to work on the project.

It was arranged that he be given the drawings and related background information necessary to acquaint him with the project. After reviewing them, he again stated his belief he could accomplish the work in a short period of time. And that is just what happened. The design work was accomplished and a new prototype provided in ten days. In addition, other changes were incorporated in the design and these were also approved.

The large company was so impressed with this job that

How to Select Products

they gave the small business a production order for some of their other requirements. From this original order has grown a very profitable and stable relationship. The small businessman was able to move quickly on something new that was advantageous. There was no innovation—creative work in incorporating the desired new features, perhaps, but no innovation.

The inventory and manufacturing work which the small business undertook as the result of the orders resulting from the ability to move quickly were not subject to the same fatal error as the new parts that would not fit anything. The comparison of the success of the ice-making company and the failure of the electronics parts company rests primarily on the distinction I have tried to make. On the one hand, the work was done on an established product; on the other, the work that was done required that more new work be done on other parts of the device before it could even be considered.

One of the best financial officers I ever knew coined a word for the inventory a business may find itself with—SMOOSI, meaning Slow Moving, Obsolete and Off Standard Inventory. To me the word is almost onomatopoetic. It has been my experience that, with the exception of inventories that have a quality defect, most inventories that eventually are written off or scrapped have developed out of the attempts by small businessmen to innovate.

Guideline number 14 is: *Your small size is of special disadvantage in handling inventories. Do not confuse the ability to move quickly with the ability to innovate. Inventories of products that represent some aspect of innovation are the most susceptable of all classes of merchandise to becoming worthless. Pick products that tend, as much as possible, to insulate your small business from this risk.*

Several times in this chapter and the one preceding it I have mentioned the idea of value added. No discussion of product, service, manufacturing process or design would be

How to Select Products

complete without mention being made of one of my pet complaints with accepted management thinking. I refer to what is known as a "cost reduction program."

The term is widely used and is descriptive of programs aimed at eliminating or reducing the costs associated with making a product, selling a product or even of operating an entire business. I have no confidence in such programs because they start from the premise of examining costs with a view to their reduction. *This is wrong*.

Any business for profit, large or small, exists for the sole purpose of *spending money*. In doing this they must *create value* in excess of the money they spend. They must create this value in such a way that someone else (the customer) will pay for it. That is the economic process on which the free enterprise system is based.

Therefore, when you are contemplating the products your small business will make or sell or the services you will provide, think about them in these terms. *Do not* plan your operations, particularly your internal manufacturing operations, starting from the assumption that costs are "bad" and should be reduced. The conclusion of a completely successful cost reduction program—i.e., the elimination of all costs—will result in no money being spent, hence no business.

Take each area where you are now spending or plan to spend money. Without thinking about eliminating the cost, ask yourself if the same amount of money spent for something else would add as much profit, create as much value in excess of the costs. If the answer is "yes," then you will have an easy decision. If your answer is "no," then the reverse is true.

You will soon discover that a regular analysis of your business in this fashion will lead you to emphasize the profitable ways to spend money and eliminate the unprofitable. This is nowhere more true in any business than in the area

How to Select Products

we have considered in this chapter—the product or service you are selling. This is the area where proper analysis will add the most profit to your operations.

Guideline number 15 is:

Your small business exists for the purpose of spending money to add value above your costs. This increment of value is your profit. Look at your spending, not with the purpose of eliminating it, but with the purpose of finding ways to spend the same amount to create more value.

Every now and then, a small company will have the situation of greatly reduced volume forced upon it overnight. This is always a great shock to any organization and the way the owner-manager or president reacts may well determine whether the small business will have a future or not.

There is only one thing to do. The operation must immediately be cut back to a size that is consistent with the remaining volume. Even though it will be the hardest thing in the world to do, the small businessman faced with a large loss of volume must cut immediately. In my experience, the small businessmen who have not acted quickly have eventually failed, and those who have acted quickly have all survived.

When this situation of greatly reduced volume comes up suddenly, the temptation is to keep the staff intact while replacement volume is being obtained. The fallacy in the temptation is that the additional volume is not attainable, otherwise it would have been gotten already. I have seen good men go down to the most ignominious disaster by thrashing around desperately to "get that big order" while their overhead was eating them up. Sometimes, in his desperation, the small businessman thus driven will take on business at lower prices just to get some volume in the house. The only difference this makes is that losses may occur more slowly.

The temptation not to cut back is infinitely stronger when there is a much slower attrition. It has always seemed to me curious that bad news received in little doses does not have

How to Select Products

the same effect as bad news received in a large dose. Bad news is bad news no matter what the amount and how received. The effects of a gradual decline in volume are equally as serious as an instantaneous loss. The need for cutting back is still present but is aggravated by the difficulty of knowing how far the decline will go and thus how far to cut back. The insidious nature of this situation rests on the fact that procrastination regarding corrective action is so easily rationalized by a wait-and-see attitude.

I recall a situation where just such events had taken place over a period of six years. The small business in question was a manufacturer of electronic parts. They had been purchased by a large company and were run as a separate division for a period of nearly six years. During that time volume had very gradually declined while no attempt was made to cut back the staff and otherwise trim the operation to a size that would produce profits at the lower rates of sales.

The income statement of this small business showed the results of this trend. When purchased by the large concern, the company had a sales volume of about $3.5 million and had averaged post-tax profits over the preceding three years of approximately $300,000 per year. During the intervening six years sales had fallen to $2.5 million and the last year the small business lost $250,000.

I became involved when another company with a similar line of products came in to see us with the idea of our helping them acquire another company in their line. The division run by the large concern was one logical candidate, and after investigation and negotiation a deal was made whereby my company would put up some cash, the large concern would take notes, and the division would be purchased by our client.

Shortly before the closing, the president of our client company came in to see me and outlined his plan for integrating the two companies. Among his plans, and as a first step, he

How to Select Products

proposed to make the division of the large concern profitable on its own. His method was simple. He would do what any small businessman would do if he faced a sudden loss of sales of about the same magnitude as the division's sales had declined gradually over the six years. He would cut back his staff immediately.

Therefore, the day after the closing he and I went out to the newly acquired operation and spent the day drawing up an organization chart. We wrote down the names of each employee and a brief description of what he did. We did not know any of the employees so we relied on the general manager to give us a brief account of each employee's abilities and job performance. There were, at the time, 138 employees in total.

That night we went over the lists and charts by ourselves, and the next day, back at the plant, we discharged 40 employees, reduced the pay of six more, and instituted partial days in certain departments. We were as fair as we could be and gave each discharged employee two weeks' severance pay. We set up a job assistance program to help them get relocated. Those employees who remained we called into a meeting to tell them what we had done and why it had been necessary to do it if any jobs were to be saved.

Of course there was a period of unrest. But the company made a profit that first month and has made profits every month since then. We kept the employees informed and the news of a profit was a shot in the arm. The plant produced more goods at a better quality standard with a third less employees. Soon morale was at an all-time high.

Guideline number 16 is:

As a small business you must react immediately to bring expenses into line with a volume decline. A gradual decline, as compared to an immediate one, will be more difficult to handle in a program of cut-backs because it will be hard to know how far the decline will go. A disadvantage of your small size is that you will be unable to afford the luxury of

How to Select Products

keeping up your staff because you will probably be unable to predict the extent or the duration of the decline with sufficient accuracy to know the extent of your losses.

One word of caution and a reflective thought should be made in closing. The caution is that while it is the essence of a business that it *spend* money, many people get carried away and lose touch with reality the minute they have any real money to spend. The old saying that so-and-so "couldn't stand prosperity" was invented to describe these people. I talked earlier about discipline. The discipline a man shows in the way he spends money is the very best test of his character.

The reflection is whimsical, but it is one that I nonetheless enjoy. I have often wondered what a small businessman would do if he had to pay for the things he buys for his business on a simple barter basis. For example, suppose he had a salesman who was being paid $15,000 a year in salary. Would the small businessman think more about this amount if he had to pay the man his wages with, say, 200 shares of Proctor & Gamble stock, or three Cadillac convertibles, or a small Matisse, or one magnificent Oriental rug, or 60,000 bars of soap?

I sometimes try to discover what it is that would strike a man as unreasonable, even though the cost—the amount of money spent—would be the same. This is the theory of "opportunity cost" propounded by Thorstein Veblen long ago. It seeks to determine the value a man places on something expressed in terms of something besides money.

There is this last to say about the products or services a small business may manufacture or provide. Whatever your product or service is, your selection of it will determine the kind of people you will be working with. I have always found it useful to really look at the type of people who seem to be characteristic of the trade they are practicing. If you are thinking about getting into a business, take a look at the people you meet who are now in it. If you are already in

How to Select Products

business, take a look at your fellows. Think also about what kind of people used to be in that trade in the past. Whatever the trend, whatever you observe the present inhabitants of that business to be, rest assured of one thing; you will be or probably already are very much like them.

5

How to Manage Your Small Business

Every now and then this country finds itself with a political leader who is also a great phrasemaker. President Harry S. Truman was such, and whenever I think of all the problems that beset the man who has undertaken to run his own small business, I am reminded of one of his very quotable quotes: "If you can't stand the heat, get out of the kitchen."

That is true of the small business operator. The pressure on this man will be more than he ever expected. That is why in the first chapter of this book I said that there was only one valid reason for starting your own business—a compulsion to undertake the task, a feeling that there is no other way available to do the things you want to do.

Let me say again that I believe this so completely that once I am convinced a man is in small business for that reason, I will spend as much of my own efforts as I can to help him. And that applies even if there is no chance of my company's financing his operation. Quite aside from its being good business, in that it builds good will for my company in the small business community, I *want* to help this man.

Actually, the small businessman deserves better help than he can get from me, but I offer it nonetheless. He deserves help because he has undertaken to build a business, to create an enterprise in his own image. This, to my way of thinking, entitles him to all the help any man can give him, especially if one understands as I do the problems he will have to master if he is to be a success.

When it comes to managing a small business, the most difficult of these problems will be faced. There is no magic way to make the management of a small business a simple matter, because the *management has already been picked.* Remember that I previously pointed out that the most important decision a small businessman may make is in selecting the president or manager of his business—and it is usually *himself.*

Therefore, although I do not know how to manage any particular small business without having first-hand knowledge of its affairs, I propose here to make some observations about the nature of small business and small size as it applies to that indistinct art called management.

I call it an indistinct art because that is just what it is. My bookshelf is bending under the weight of writings on management, and many of them are quite helpful in getting the "feel" of what it is to practice the art. I have spent nearly a third of my business life in positions where I was involved in writing and lecturing on the subject, and I took a master's degree in Business Administration. In short, I should know what management is if anyone does.

But I do *not* know what it is. The closest I ever came to understanding what business management is all about was during the years I was teaching it. Indeed, there are many things in this world that can best be learned by trying to teach them to someone else. Management of a business is one of them, and that is my first general consideration:

Whenever you think you understand something about your small business, try to teach it to someone else, such as an employee, another small businessman or even your wife. It will improve your own understanding.

How to Manage Your Small Business

I have heard so many different analogies of what being the president of a small business is like that I have thrown away the lists which I used to keep. The one I like best compares the small business president to an orchestra leader.

The analogy begins with the various sections of the orchestra—strings are customers, woodwinds are manufacturing, percussion is finance, etc. The president or manager is the orchestra leader who has several essential tasks:

1. He selects the pieces the orchestra will play.

2. He sees that all the players are equipped with a score and have the instruments required.

3. He *directs* their play and *determines* the interpretation of what they play.

Later on in this chapter I will try to point out some of the things that can be done to gain control of your small business, or to regain it if you have lost control. Before doing that, however, I want to make a few observations about the nature of control as a state or condition that exists at any one time in a small business.

Consider again our analogy:

1. *The conductor selects the pieces the orchestra will play.* Believe me when I tell you that most small businessmen *do not* have that kind of control over their business. It is one of the most common complaints of a small businessman that his company seems to be running him. One thing or another happens and the small businessman finds himself running his business for purposes other than he chose or he finds himself making decisions that are dictated by requirements over which he has no control. Sometimes when this control is lost, the penalty can be as severe and complete as the loss of the small business itself.

Several examples have already been mentioned in earlier contexts. The man with the chemical manufacturing process never did have control of his business. When he had gotten his production facility operating, he could not sell the volume of production the plant was geared to make. He could run the plant only part-time while he was getting additional sales, and when his sales efforts resulted in the influx of a large amount of business his plant was then not capable of making enough chemical. This man never had any real control over his business.

There is another point that must be made here. Referring back to my comments on the time-span of decision-making, and the necessity of making decisions at one point in time that will be implemented at a future time, it can be seen from the example that this businessman, being in the process-type of manufacturing business and thus in the largest time-span category, was doubly incapable of regaining control. First, the plant would overproduce against his sales, then it would underproduce against his increased sales.

The degree of control, or call it management's ability to direct the company's affairs, must be more complete the longer the time-span of decision-making. The ability of management to correct an out-of-control situation depends in part on the flexibility it has. Time is an important factor in determining such flexibility.

2. *All the players must be equipped with a score and they must have the required instruments.* That is the same as saying that every employee must have a precise knowledge of how he fits into the overall scheme of things and must have the required tools at hand. It implies that he will know how to use the tools.

But it is more than that. There is no more precise "plan" of anything, in terms of time, than a musical score. Just as in any music there is a precise time for each instrument to play its part, so in small business there is a precise time that appropriate activities must take place. I mention the importance of time again because it makes little difference if the musician can play his instrument well or poorly, or an employee is a good or poor purchasing agent, if he does not perform his part *on time.*

In a previous chapter I mentioned the sad plight of a

company that developed a new line of products that sat on the shelf because *they were ahead of time.* The company's engineer, who was also the owner-president, developed a line of products that was nearly five years ahead of the industry's ability to use it. The products might just as well have been five years late for all the good they did the company.

It is, therefore, not enough that certain functions within the business be accomplished on time. The business itself must be so directed that it, too, performs on time. There are so many instances of this that it does not need to be illustrated. Orders must go out—on time. Bills must be paid—on time. Raw materials must be obtained—on time. In short, the small business manager's sense of timing is as important an ingredient in his success as any single ability. Even if he does all else well and thoroughly, if his timing is off, much of the good work will be wasted.

3. *They must rehearse and play under the conductor's direction and following his intrepretation.* This is the same as saying that over and above the manager's responsibility to determine the course of his company (selecting the numbers to be played) and to adequately equip his employees with training and tools (providing the music and the instruments to capable musicians), the small business manager must also interpret the company's plans, much as an orchestra leader must interpret, for example, a Bach concerto.

By this I mean that it is up to the small business manager to breathe life and vitality into his plans and give them direction and purpose. There is nothing in my experience quite so sad as having a businessman tell how all his plans came to nothing. Usually it was because, having made the plans, the business manager promptly forgot them and went about his job haphazardly. There are also many small businessmen who are either unwilling or emotionally unable to follow a plan.

Moses, although he is not remembered as an early practi-

How to Manage Your Small Business

tioner of organization, nevertheless was responsible for drawing up the first table of organization. You will recall the Tribes of Israel had wandered through the deserts of the Middle East for many years following their expulsion from Egypt. Then came Moses, who organized the Tribes on a units of ten basis as follows: ten people to a unit; ten units reporting to a unit chief; ten unit chiefs reporting to a unit chiefs' chief; etc. With the Tribes thus organized Moses led them into Israel in a matter of months.

In more modern times, I was once asked to join the board of directors of a company that was in the consumer soft goods line. In looking over the company prior to giving my answer, I observed that plans were always made at the beginning of each season and then filed away. Management did nothing in the way of telling their employees about the plans. Each fall, the management would get together and spend a long week-end at a resort in the Catskills. From this weekend would come a plan for the coming year. Upon returning to New York, the management would immediately go about making all kinds of decisions with no regard to the plan. An even greater difficulty was imposed because various members of management would actually make some decisions *based on the plan,* thereby creating real chaos.

On the other hand I was for four years a director of a company that over the past three years accomplished a remarkable record of progress. All of it was based on a plan prepared by management and then followed to the letter. The program called for many things which presented difficulty in execution. Once, because the plan demanded that each of the company's product lines be made to stand on its own and contribute profits, it became necessary to drop an established line that could not be priced adequately to provide a profit. Sales declined as a result. However, profits were larger on the remaining sales.

If you will look at the men you know who are in small

[118]

business, you will notice that some of them seem to be on a never-ending treadmill of one crisis after another. They will complain that cash is very tight, or that competition is cutting into their sales, or that they cannot get enough help. There will always be something.

Then there will be those who seem always to have events under their control. These are the small business operators who also have problems but who seem to have ways of dealing with them. It is no accident they are thus situated. They have, without even being aware of it perhaps, gotten their small business organized and are managing it according to some plan.

One more word of caution before I continue. There are as many different ways to manage a small business as there are small businessmen. Every man I know has his own "style" and emphasizes certain aspects of his management more than others, all according to his personality and objectives. What I propose to do in this chapter is to set forth some thoughts concerning the process of management. As in the previous chapters, I will try to say what I have to in a way sufficiently general for anyone to adapt it to his own situation.

When you take the time to think about your business—and you *must* take the time to do it occasionally—you will observe that your job of managing is really the job of manipulating a series of events and a number of different people making and selling your product or service. Your job as manager gives you the responsibility, for example, of providing the work area for your plant or store, having it adequately staffed with workers to accomplish the required tasks, seeing to it that funds are available to pay the wages and bills, getting the customers to buy—the whole range of things that go into the cycle of your business.

Thus we have here the second general consideration:
The manager's job in a small business is first to create and then to direct a whole series of relationships between his

How to Manage Your Small Business

company and its employees, suppliers, bankers, and customers.

I say *create* and *direct* because in a small business, particularly a new small business, these relationships are not ready-made and already well-established, as is the case in a larger company.

The first step in creating the desired relationships is *to set objectives*. It is in this process that many small businessmen fail themselves miserably; in fact, many small businessmen I have known do not even pay themselves the courtesy of setting objectives for themselves. While they may try to direct the work of others along certain lines, they do not sit down with themselves and go through the process of setting objectives.

They thus fail themselves in a way they would never forgive in another man who was their boss. People have a right to know what is expected of them, and I have always thought that a man would do better work if he knew what it was he was working toward. This is the first point in the managers job of setting objectives: *Always discuss the objectives you wish to impose with the people who will be expected to attain them.*

There is a double benefit in discussing objectives with your employees. In so doing you will not only educate them as to the reason for their part in the program, you will also be setting for them a goal against which you can later measure their performance. Thus, the second point: *Objectives should be set in such a way that the results of achievement can be stated in measurable terms.*

There is nothing quite so disturbing to an employee as being second-guessed by his boss. If you set out your objectives so that the results can be easily measured, then the employee will know all the time as he is working away at his job just how he is doing. This will also be of great value to the manager when he appraises each man's work.

It is important that progress toward each objective be stated in measurable terms. Indeed, the stated objective is not completely defined unless progress toward it is subject to measurement. Objectives must be precise and part of the precision is obtained by defining the point at which the objective has been attained. Again, this is always the manager's job.

Consider, on the one hand, an imprecise and fuzzy objective such as "increasing sales." You can believe me when I tell you that this objective is typical of the planning done by many small businessmen. It is not really an objective in any sense of the word as I am using it here. It is more like wishful thinking, fuzzy dreaming, and it is certainly poor management.

On the other hand, consider an objective stated as follows: "The company has the objective of increasing its sales by a minimum of 10 per cent and a maximum of 20 per cent over the next 12 months at prices which will provide a gross profit of 35 per cent." This is an objective a salesman can sink his teeth into. He has a specified amount of sales to provide, he has an idea about the pricing of his products or services and he has a time period established in which to achieve his objectives. He is provided also with a means of knowing absolutely how he is doing at any one time, and when his appraisal review comes up he won't be surprised. He knows he either made it or he didn't.

But one thing is sure: The conditions which were present at the time the objectives were set will not be the conditions which prevail throughout any time period provided in the objectives. In the example of sales objectives, there are so many things that can happen during a year's time that it would be impossible to list them. You can think of many yourself, such as price reductions by the competition, lack of materials or personnel required to make the product or provide the services, etc. In any case, point number three is:

How to Manage Your Small Business

Changing circumstances will unquestionably affect the plans laid in connection with the objectives. Be sure to provide a means for modifying objectives to meet such changes.

There is one additional point to remember when you are setting objectives. Typical of what happens when this point is overlooked is the problem faced by a man who came into my office about a year ago. For some years he had been engaged in the manufacture of specialized valves for marine applications. He had set as an objective for his company specialization in steam valves and valves to control the flow of high pressure water.

This policy worked very well for several years. Gradually, however, sales began to show a decline although the company knew they were getting their historic share of the market and were actually getting some business away from their competition. Profits during this period were the highest in the company's history due chiefly to the lack of any program and related expense directed toward developing other products.

The president-owner of this small business came in to see me at a time when his company's sales had further declined to a point where operations were just barely in the black. He said to me that he had stuck to his objective of specializing in his line of marine valves much too long. His profits had convinced him that his policy was the correct one, but now even his profits were about to disappear.

Unfortunately for the man, he had not kept these profits in his business. Rather he had drawn them out in salaries and bonuses. The result was a company that had a shrinking market and no funds with which to get into another line. We declined the chance to finance this company. But the lesson was clear. There had been much evidence available to indicate the need to re-evaluate the objective of specialization, but this evidence was not acted upon because of the current profits the company was generating. The objective was not considered in terms of the future profitability of the company. Therefore, point number four is: *You must constantly test your objectives—and the policies established to implement progress toward them—in terms of the long-range profitability of the company. Activities that appear profitable today may not be so in the future.*

There are many refinements which are standard procedures when larger companies set objectives. Books have been written on the subject. For the small businessman, however, the four points I have mentioned are the most important. If they are followed, a good basic job will have been done of laying out in an orderly way the future goals toward which the company will work.

The trouble with so many small businessmen is that they seldom set objectives for themselves in any meaningful form. Since they have no objectives worthy of the name, their employees are even more in the dark. But that is not all! An even larger problem with many small businessmen is that they do not *organize*. They characteristically seem to pass up organization planning as something only a large company can afford. Nothing could be further from the truth.

I try to be understanding of the un-organized small businessmen. I am willing to overlook this fault because of the kinds of men who go into a small business. They are usually the "doers"; they are men of an aggressive nature as contrasted with men who are not primarily men of action. In such men I can understand the inability to sit down in a quiet room and draw up a plan of organization.

In my experience, the organization of the typical small business is developed as a matter of accomodation to circumstances. The small business owner has got to be the prime mover in his company. Most of the things that have to be done are done either by himself or under his direct supervision. This is particularly true during the early years of a small business. It is to be expected that a man thus engaged will not have the inclination to apply the tested principles of organization to his business when they are required as the result of growth, and the ultimate point is reached where it is more than he or any man can do to run the whole show.

Indeed, many small businesses I know will always be small. They may be profitable, they may be stable, they may be well-financed, but they will remain small for one of two reasons. The owner may be incapable of delegating any authority (the first and most difficult step in organization planning), whether he understands his need to do so or not, or he may well understand the need to delegate but be unwilling to do it. In the latter case, since it is his business, he has, according to my view, every right to make this decision.

We once financed a very small company at the earliest stages of its corporate life. From a modest beginning the company grew in sales and profits until it reached a plateau of about $250,000 annual sales value. This was the point in that particular company which the president could not pass and still keep every detail under his control. We had many conversations, that president and I, about what to do. It was decided to move ahead. Accordingly the president hired an engineer to work with him. In a period of a year he had hired and fired three men. His trouble was that, being the owner of the business, very aggressive, hard-working, and having great talent, the man expected his newly hired engineers to show the same traits. During that year it became obvious to him—through much prodding from me, I must admit—that he would have to settle for good work from these men and not expect the same superb work of which he himself was capable.

His decision was to cut back. During the "year of the engineers," as we called it, sales had increased to $400,000 and were profitable. Following the dismissal of the last engineer, sales were cut back to the lower level and the president seemed to accept the situation. He was content to get back complete control of his business, and once again have his hand in everything.

How to Manage Your Small Business

But the story did not end there. After less than a year of reduced operations he called me on the phone one evening at home. He said he had been doing a lot of thinking and wanted to see me right away. It was, and is, typical of the man that, having reached a decision, he called me immediately. I am sure he would have done so if it had been midnight; actually it was about 8:30 P.M.

I agreed to meet him at a restaurant midway between our two homes. I would have agreed to meet this man any place at any time because he is one of the best small businessmen I know. In any case, he said that all of his thinking had led him to the conclusion that he must build his company, and if that meant holding himself in check and being more tolerant of his employees' failures to hit excellence every time, then that is what he was now ready to do.

So this small businessman had gone through the complete cycle. He first stayed at the plateau of his own ability to be the sole decision-maker. Then he tried building an organization and failed. He returned to the first plateau. In the two years since his decision to try to build up his company the second time, his employees have tripled in number and his sales and profits have increased fourfold.

I once asked him what had made him change his mind the second time around. "It was easy," he said. "I came to the conclusion I was more at fault than they [the engineers] were and that my mistake was worse than anything they did."

In any case, there is a time in every small business when the manager will have to give the responsibility for some decision-making to someone else. It is at that point that the small businessman begins to practice what is called *organization*. And, just as there were a few helpful points in setting objectives, so are there a few concerning this task of management.

The next point follows from the circumstances surrounding the development of the need for organization. As the small business grows, the manager becomes more and more removed from the place where, and the point in time when, decisions must be made. Or he may not be removed in the sense of being "distant"; it may be simply a case of being "removed" by the press of other work which also requires his time and attention. Decisions are best made by the man closest to the spot. The fifth point, then, is: *As much as possible, decision-making should be delegated to the person most closely associated with the responsibility for executing or accomplishing the task.*

Earlier I recommended that when the small businessman was setting his objectives, he should do so in such a way as to bring his employees into the discussions. If he has done this, the next point in building his organization is easily accomplished. This is the need for *writing it down.*

Did you ever try to do business with a man who never writes anything down? My experience with such men has been totally discouraging. For one thing, anytime they feel like changing their minds, they just go ahead and do it. But not if it's written down. When it is "on paper," as they say, changes can still be made, but they are not unilateral and all parties get to see the changes.

Point number six is: *As you delegate decision-making, it is essential that the employee have a written statement of his responsibilities, authority and relationships.*

Further to that point, it is not enough that the employee who is being given some decision-making authority be told what it is he can do. He should also be told what it is he cannot or should not do. And, if there are to be any exceptions to these rules, they must also be spelled out. They must be spelled out in such a way that the employee understands his relationships with the other aspects of the business and how his particular area of responsibility fits into the over-all picture. My strong recommendation is that this always *be done in writing.* And, since it is certain that conditions will change, provision must be made in the written statement of responsibility to provide for such changes.

How to Manage Your Small Business

Lest anyone think that this is all beginning to sound very much like a lot of paperwork, I can assure all concerned that, even though it is essential, it need not be burdensome. The physical act of writing something down will make the whole program clearer to the writer and will tend to avoid misinterpretation on the part of the employee.

I was once associated with a company that had highly technical machine shop practices under the direction of a foreman who was completely competent, but the most literal man I ever knew. One day I had gotten a new rug for my office and I wanted something to go under the casters of my desk chair to keep them from wearing down the rug. I spoke to the foreman on my way through his department the next day and asked him if he could get me something *flat and smooth*. "How about a piece of metal?" he said. "I have some scrap plate left over from a job." I remarked that that sounded excellent.

Several days later I came into my office after lunch and there was my chair pad. It was the nicest thing I ever saw. Then I looked on my desk and there was a time slip from that department showing total hours of work on the chair pad. At our cost, that pad ran well over $450. I nearly died.

But there was a reason for the cost. Flat to that foreman meant a piece with an average deviation of less than .001 per cent, and smooth meant a similarly very high degree of polish. The piece of scrap steel plate was worth a maximum of $5.00. The rest was labor to make it *flat and smooth*.

I believe that if I had written down what I wanted and then gone over it with the foreman, he would have understood better what I wanted and I would have understood the terms he was using.

Which brings me to the next point. I could not hold the foreman responsible for making my chair pad flat and smooth according to my instructions as he understood them. It is not my own personal style of managing to criticize someone who has not had his instructions and responsibilities written down for him and otherwise adequately explained. When I want to be critical of a man's work I like to begin by knowing that *he* knew what was expected of him. And while there are many small businessmen I know who don't follow this practice, it is nonetheless the one I strongly recommend.

The ultimate responsibility for results will always come back to the boss. It is he who has to see to it that every employee understands what he is to do, and how and when and under what circumstances. If the president or owner-manager of the small business has not seen to this task, then he himself is responsible for any failures. If the president has done this and the employee still does not turn in acceptable performance, then the boss is responsible for putting the wrong man in the job.

No matter how you may care to phrase it, there is one thing which cannot be delegated. So point number seven is: *Final accountability for results cannot be delegated.*

In his daily routines, the manager of a small business is setting an example. The kind of man his employees think he is will very largely determine their own attitude about the business. If the manager really cares about his small business it will show and it will foster the same feeling on the part of his employees more than anything else he can do.

It is the manager's job to guide the company. If he has been careless in his approach and not attentive to detail, if he has failed to provide his employees with even the simplest of objectives and if he has not taken the time to provide those employees who have some decision-making responsibility with a written statement, no matter how brief, of what is expected of them, then that manager has not provided himself with the tools he will need to guide the company.

I say that because the very purpose of guiding something, particularly a small business, is to give direction. Thus, the orchestra leader of our earlier analogy does not play all the instruments. He may not play even one, although it is not uncommon to have a band leader also featured as a musician. He probably did not make the musical arrangements. He almost certainly did not make any of the musical instruments. But he saw to it that they were all provided, and his function was to direct the assembled musicians to make music.

The first step in a manager's job of providing leadership is to encourage self-discipline by the employees. This is not possible unless he has provided them with a means of knowing what they must do. And in discussing the job to be done, I have always felt there were several basic ingredients prerequisite to getting the kind of cooperation that results in self-discipline.

The employee must:

a) Believe he can actually accomplish the assignment, physically and mentally.

b) Believe he has the tools and other equipment necessary to get the job done.

c) Believe it is in *his own best interests* to do it.

d) Believe he will get support if he runs into trouble.

When I have been able to assure myself that a man under my direction believes, truthfully, the above four things, then I know I will have a good job done with a maximum of cooperation from the employee.

Point number eight is: *Encourage self-guidance and self-discipline by your employees rather than exercise direct control. Remember that as manager or boss your personal example will be important.*

In order that an employee be able, by himself, to maintain a high level of productivity against objectives, I recommend point number nine: *Be sure that your written statement of responsibility and objective has also provided the means for the employee to measure his own performance.*

It will be necessary for the manager to appraise his employees on a regular basis if he is to know how his programs are being carried out. The work he will have done if he has

How to Manage Your Small Business

followed the line I have thus far outlined will equip him for this job.

There is nothing more annoying and upsetting to an employee, myself included, than to have his performance judged against the individual performance of another man. That is the whole purpose of having established an understanding with the employee—the avoidance of having to appraise his work against another man's and the provision of means for an appraisal on the only acceptable basis.

Point number ten is: *Always appraise performance using the previously agreed-upon objectives. Never appraise performance against performance.*

The process of management has often seemed to me to be a self-regenerating task. That is to say, having gone through all the steps from planning, to organizing, to guiding and appraising performance, it is necessary to start all over again. Perhaps it may not be self-regenerating so much as never-ending. One year's sales forecast, one year's equipment needs are superseded by the next year's. Plans are made and changed and made again. There seems to be, on the one hand, a cycle that takes place, and, on the other, a never-ending panoply of change with no beginning and no end.

This is not the case when it comes to appraising the work a man has done. If the appraisal is properly handled, he will have had a written statement of his responsibilities, the objectives he was expected to achieve and the time he was given to do the work. His appraisal must, therefore, be limited to the time under discussion, and that means *just the one time period,* whatever it might be for that particular employee.

Point number 11 is: *Performance should be appraised only during the time specified for the employee. There can be no carry-overs or carry-backs to future or past periods. Each appraisal must be limited to the agreed or stated time period.*

This has the salutary effect of wiping the slate clean after each appraisal. The employee will know that any deficiencies noted in past performance reviews will not be brought out of the closet to haunt him—provided, of course, they have been corrected. There is something encouraging to both the appraiser and the appraised in starting a fresh, new deal after each session.

For this reason, and if your company bases its pay scales on performance, point number 12 is: *Reward or correction should follow the performance review as closely as possible.*

The job of a manager will inevitably be involved with much more than I have discussed thus far. Indeed, my remarks have applied only to what goes on inside his small business. What I have tried to do is provide a few points that can serve as a minimum and which, in my view, would be adequate for the majority of small businesses.

The hard part comes when the manager, having, hopefully, satisfied himself concerning the internal management practices of his company, takes a look out the window and sees a world full of competitors, government regulations, taxes, customers who won't pay, suppliers who won't sell for anything but cash in advance, and banks that won't lend him any money.

If he is smart, our small business manager will be worried, and rightly so, because out there is the jungle and his competitors, who want to *eat him up.*

I have a number of friends who hold positions of responsibility at several of the country's leading graduate schools of business administration. They tell me that many young men who would like to apply for their courses do not do so because they feel they could not be "ethical" and be in business. They want to do something worthwhile for their fellow men, and feel that being in business would not be right, would not help them toward this goal.

One time I had the chance to spend an evening with such a group of young men. They were top-notch people. They had good marks, were active in sports and were participating

How to Manage Your Small Business

in student government activities. Several of them devoted a few nights every month to a settlement house program and others were active in the student church associations. They asked me questions about what it was like to be a small businessman.

My impression of the young men was the very highest. They were motivated to achieve all kinds of good works. They were industrious. They were thoughtful.

But my understanding of what was bothering them about business was as disturbing to me as my impression of them was comforting. Apparently they thought that everyone was entitled to security. They described their idea of security as freedom from hunger and want, freedom of religion, etc. They felt they would not make good businessmen because they would, as businessmen, have to discharge someone or promote someone over another man who needed the raise more, or take sales away from a competitor, thereby causing hardships on all the competitors' employees, and so forth.

To them, there were no easy equities in business. They viewed it as a fierce, competitive battleground where the victor won at the expense of the loser. They could not reconcile this with their personal desires to live a life of giving help and assistance to their fellow men.

I think they were probably right in their decision to stay out of business, particularly small business. It is no place for anyone who is not a competitor. I know they were wrong in their analysis of *why* business was not for them.

They formed a sort of club. Membership was open to everyone. The emphasis was on getting ready for the Peace Corps, working in slum areas, joining the poverty program, and the like. These are all programs for dedicated people, people who are competitors in the sense they are fighters for what they believe. But this club has yet to spawn its first practicing, actual member of any of these worthwhile programs. The going was too tough. Most of the men went on to do various graduate work to further equip themselves to live in the world of ideas and thoughts.

How to Manage Your Small Business

I do not mean to be critical, for these, too, are worthwhile objectives. The point is that the spirit of competition and the need to be strong enough and have sufficient courage to stand up and fight are prerequisite qualities for other careers as well as for the small businessman. That is why the young men were wrong; there is fierce competition everywhere.

It is when he sits and looks out the window and sees the competitive world in which he is going to make his mark and his company's mark that the small businessman gets down to the nub of the question, "How can I best compete?"

I happen to have some words of comfort for him, provided he will follow a few simple suggestions and has the desire to compete. He will find that most people in small business are not concerned with him, do not spend attention to detail and are not really interested in making their decisions based on an analysis of the competition. Probably they are too busy putting out all their own brush fires. The alert small business operator, therefore, will have a good chance if he is careful, cautious, is aware of his competition and *manages his own company accordingly.*

One of the best examples of what can go wrong when a man runs his company without giving regard to this most important aspect of small business happened to a company of which I was a director. Much of the blame should go to me for forgetting this point—in fact, double blame because I fell privy to some information that would have been helpful in avoiding the problem.

The company manufactures a line of industrial equipment that is highly engineered and is made up of sub-component parts supplied by other manufacturers. One of the company's principal competitors was reported to be falling behind in the development of its products and much of its line was considered to be several years behind the trade. The company with which I was associated had a regular program of product improvement, and, quite frankly, we all felt the competitor could never catch up. We therefore made plans merely to continue our existing program and not try to make any giant steps in product improvement. In this business it typically required 12 to 18 months to get from a product design change to the point where the change was incorporated in the whole line of the company's products.

Then one day I was asked by a friend if I had ever heard of the such-and-such company, the competitor company. I said that of course I knew of them. My friend then said that a relative of his had recently come over from the old country and had gone to work for them. That was all.

A year later, the competitor came on the market with a line of products that made our line obsolete in many important respects. In discussing his grave situation at a board meeting, the president told of how the competitor had hired a man who was considered the industry's genius.

You have already guessed it. It was the same man, my friend's relative. If I had known enough to tell the president, that would have been the signal to look further. As it later turned out, I was not the only one who had come across other bits of information that pieced together would have told the story.

For example, the company's purchasing agent had been asked by one of our suppliers why the competitor had stopped buying one kind of material and begun buying another. Again, a salesman of ours had been talking to a customer who had asked if we knew why the competitor had refused to make shipment commitments to its customers on certain of its products beyond a certain date.

To summarize, there was ample information available to our company to have predicted the move our competitor was going to make at least six months before the new products were introduced. In addition, it was all available at no extra work other than making it known to our company's management.

With all his problems of being limited in many areas, the small businessman is especially vulnerable to a bold move by the competition. If he is to avoid this type of problem he must, in addition to managing his company well internally, make provision to keep himself informed about his competition and provide himself with the means of predicting, as closely as possible, what his competition will do. He must then make his own plans for his own company on his thus more complete understanding.

We had a game we used to play as children in which we would try to make the perfect wish to accomplish whatever specified objective we had before us. My father called it the "I Wish Game." He used to tell us, and it was not until much later in my life that I understood what he had meant, that if your objective is to achieve power, the best possible wish would be for next month's edition of the Sunday *New York Times*.

He was right, of course; knowledge is the real power. The knowledge of what will actually take place a month in advance would be enough to give any man all the power he could use.

How can a small businessman provide himself and his company with the next best thing—an educated guess?

Again, there is much written on this subject, but you won't find it in the listings under management. Look under the listings on the strategy of games, on the strategy of power, and so forth. As a matter of fact, I prefer the name "Strategic Program" for this type of business analysis because that is just what it is. When you have completed this kind of analysis you will have a program of strategy directed towards achieving your goals within the framework of the competitive aspects of your small business.

Let me begin my remarks on this aspect of your job as manager of a small business by telling what a strategic program *is not*. It is not making careful plans for marketing, production, finance, etc. These are essential prior steps and much care is required in the planning of these important considerations.

A strategic program is a program based on the position of

your small business in the whole environment of your operations. It includes the internal functional areas such as marketing, but it places the emphasis on what things your business should have in order to assure its ability to market its products profitably. The strategic program considers all the functional areas of your business in the same terms; for example, what additional plant and equipment will you need to be able to get your costs of manufacturing *below* your competitor's costs.

This type of program, therefore, requires the small businessman to learn what his competitor's costs actually are. It requires an analysis of his competitor's marketing ability in such terms that a program of strategy *can be drawn up* to get better or improved marketing capabilities for his small business.

The program also includes an analysis of what will be required to achieve a competitive advantage. This part of the program is laid out in such a way as to show the time for, and the cost of, the acquisition of required competitive tools.

Take as an example the case of a roadside hot dog stand I patronize occasionally. Within the last four years I have observed the operator of this business develop and carry out what was precisely a strategic program. I helped the man develop the program after he had applied to my company for financing. I had turned the application down, but was able to put him into a group that supplied the needed funds. During my talks with this young man, I got to like him so much that when he asked me if I would help him work up his program, I was glad to do it.

He had started his business some three months prior to his visit to me. By that time he knew what the business was like and the problems he was facing.

In this connection, we first spelled out the background. This included:

1. A statement of his basic objectives and the assumptions he was making.

How to Manage Your Small Business

2. What his present situation was.

3. What things should be handled first because they were the most troublesome.

4. What things could be handled later on because they were not as pressing as the items under number 3.

5. What things were required in terms of money, people, facilities, and time in order to accomplish the items under 3 and 4.

6. An analysis of his competitors which showed what they had at present, what he thought they might get in the future and what they had in the resources of money, people, facilities and time.

7. An estimate of what he would have to do in order to stay even with his competition, and what he would have to do to beat them.

8. A time schedule and cost estimate of the things he would have to do in order to beat the competition estimated under 7.

Let me give a few examples of how this very small business has handled the program of strategy since then. The following were among the things we wrote down.

1. Among the objectives he stated was the building of at least three more hot dog stands within five years. To achieve this goal he assumed he would be able to get financing if he could show good profits on his first stand. His assumption was that he could get a loan for one-half the cost of the second stand when the profits from his first stand could pay the interest and principal on the loan and when he had the other one-half to put up himself.

2. This tied in with his analysis of his present situation. He needed more traffic to pull into the area around his stand, which meant having a paving job done on a larger parking lot.

3. The parking lot and paving job were considered to be the first order of priority because increased business was the key to his profits on the first stand.

How to Manage Your Small Business

4. Once the lot was paved and he began getting increased volume, he thought he would hire an assistant and begin training him to run the second stand when he could open it. The man was to be hired when it was clear the first stand was going to be successful.

5. To buy the land and pay the costs of paving the lot he needed funds he did not have. Therefore, it was decided to try to get another business to move in next to him. Then there would be two businesses to share the cost, and they might help draw trade for each other.

6. There were many other road stands along the five miles of road on either side of his site. He knew most of the operators. There were also other places where a person could buy a light meal off the main highway but within a two-mile radius. He prepared a list and then ranked them according to his knowledge of what they had and what they might do in the future to hurt him. Out of a total list of 17 establishments, six other eating places represented a real threat. The one thing he thought he could do to help himself and at the same time slow down one of his six competitors was to hire away a good man from one of them when he felt he would need an assistant.

7. He estimated that a chain of three more stands within a five-mile radius of his first stand would provide him with sufficient volume and coverage to permit heavy advertising and other promotion. He estimated that he could not stay even with his competitors and still have a profitable business because of the saturation of similar light meal business in the area.

8. He estimated that it would require two years to build his first stand up to the point where he could go into the second, 18 months to get the two stands going together to get into the third stand, and a year after that to get into the fourth.

How has it worked out so far and what is the future for this man and his small business?

For nine months he looked and looked for another busi-

How to Manage Your Small Business

ness to come in near his area. There were several near-misses and it was discouraging work. Finally, a garden and home center was found that was looking for a site in that area. This business was found by a broker who operated 50 miles away but who had been contacted by this energetic young man.

The garden and home center moved in and the lot was paved. Then both businesses seemed to draw for each other as planned. The hot dog stand began to prosper; loss operations which had characterized the stand for its first year turned into good profits.

However, the losses had taken more of the man's money than he had planned. This required him to wait nearly 2½ years from the beginning before he had the one-half of the cash required for the second stand. By then, however, there was a period of tightening money and he could only get financing of one-third instead of the one-half he had thought.

This meant he had to wait another few months while he accumulated the funds. This additional period was made even longer because he had hired a man—not the one he originally had his eye on (that man had left for another job), but a good man nonetheless. Finally, he had his financing.

But in the delay he had lost the spot he wanted for his second stand and therefore decided to wait in order to get a spot that would not be subject to some of the problems he had had with the first stand. With his financing arranged he was able to move quickly when just the right location came along.

He opened his second stand one year later than he had planned. In the meantime, the six competitors about whom he had been worried had just about the same operations they had before, and he was not overly worried about the extra year.

With the acquisition of his second stand, he began a modest program of advertising and promotion. He is a great believer in billboard advertising and that is what he spent his money on. He believed in building an image for his business, so he had very distinctive dresses for his car-hops and very distinctive paint work on his stands.

The third stand went up less than 18 months after the second. The profits have been better than planned because the volume of traffic into his locations has been growing. Of the six major competitors, two have changed hands, three have gone out of business and one was torn down to make way for an interstate highway.

The man has decided to stop with three stands. He has a business that gives him a very good living. He does not aspire to build his chain any larger because he feels, based on his experience, that he can manage three but not four stands himself. He also believes that four stands might be more than his local area could adequately support.

This is just a brief overview of the planning and attention to detail that was done by this small business operator. His name will never go down in history as being the empire builder in the hot-dog-stand field, but he did a good job of *managing* his small business in his own way and he modified his objectives to fit the changing circumstances.

I give this example for two reasons. First, I want to show that a program of planning and strategy is just as appropriate for a small business as it is for a larger one. Second, I want to show how simple it really is for you to do the job of planning and then stick to the strategy you have made.

Small businessmen know what I mean when I say that the facts of business life are not always easy. There are the confinements and restrictions placed on small businesses merely because they are small. There are limits to all the categories of resources any business needs.

The fun of it is in making a success, in making plans come out, in making the competition aware of your company. The trick of it is in how well you can bring together all the ingredients, how well you manage them toward your objectives.

6

The Philosophy of a Venture Capitalist

There are many different ways to describe something—all of them depending on a point of view. For example, the city of New York could be described in a geographical sense—where it is physically located; it could be described in economic terms—what its importance is in the field of business and finance; it could be described in ethnic terms—what the backgrounds of its people are, where they were born, what languages they speak, what customs they live by; it could be described in cultural terms—what museums it has, what art is made there, what public institutions of music and the theater it supports. All of these and many more are perfectly appropriate ways to describe New York City and all it embraces.

The same is true when describing small business. There are so many points of interest, so many ways in which the total community of small business affects our daily lives that to undertake a complete analysis would require a shelf of books. It is more than can be undertaken in any one book, this one included.

My object in writing this book has been to dispel some of the misunderstanding that pervades the thinking and writ-

The Philosophy of a Venture Capitalist

ing on the subject of small business. Much of this misunderstanding I believe comes from the name itself. Small business is a name that has been used to describe a condition; it is the handle that has been attached to commercial undertakings of small size.

It is the appropriateness of this name that has somehow misled those who would write and talk about the subject. These people have started their thinking from the point of view of adapting the techniques of management used by business—i.e., big business—to small business. They have taken, for example, various organizational techniques and tried to apply them to the special problems of the small businessman. Or, they may have developed a way for a small company to apply the selling techniques of a big business.

In this they have largely missed the boat. By this I don't mean to imply that what has been written about small business has been wrong, or that the programs we have to help small business have been anything but useful. I strongly believe, however, that they have not been as universally successful as it was hoped they would be because they have not adequately prepared the small businessman to meet the problems and difficulties he will face simply because his business is small.

Further, I think they have missed their potential effectiveness because they are directed away from the really interesting and exciting aspects of small business—that is, the advantages of being small, of not being bound by tradition, of having a new idea and being able to do something about it, of not being tied down to the slow and methodical ways big organizations are forced to adapt, of being able to run a risk, take a long-shot, *make a venture* if for no other reason than to see if it will work.

If the reader of this book gets only one lasting impression for his pains, I hope it will be that there are real challenges to being small and in being a small businessman. To serve this purpose I have so far devoted my remarks to the several

The Philosophy of a Venture Capitalist

functional areas of a small business with the emphasis on special considerations arising out of the fact of smallness. I have undertaken to make my remarks sufficiently general in the hope they may thus be of use to any small businessman whether he is the principal of a small firm of architects, the proprietor of a corner grocery store, the owner of a restaurant, a manufacturer or the head of a small sales agency.

I fully realize that by being so general, a good deal has been lost. There is always an advantage in being precise, but the choice was between making my remarks more applicable to one particular type of small business—hence more useful in that area—or making them of a nature more universally applicable to any business in the happy circumstance of being small.

I stated above I thought the connotation "small business" was misleading and that much of the work done in the past on the subject had been less than 100 per cent effective. While I do not propose to recommend a change in the appellation "small business," I think it should be made clear that the term "small business" describes only the actual size of the enterprise. That is all it describes; and it is the least meaningful description in terms of the small businessman, his objectives, his feeling for his business and what things are important to him.

It is the philosophy of the small businessman that has eluded the majority of those who would help him. They have thought of him as a businessman who happens to be small, and they have been wrong. They should have thought of him as a man who may call himself a small businessman but who thinks of himself and of his business in almost any other term but "small."

To him, his business is his whole life. So whatever else it may be, it is not "small," and most small businessmen I know, myself included, would never agree that "small" is descriptive of the importance of their enterprise, or their lives. Since the business is thus such an integral part of the

The Philosophy of a Venture Capitalist

man's life and his aspirations, it represents the very best that is in him. Therefore, it is a profanity and a condescension to call it "small" except as to economic size.

To the small businessman his "small" business is a summer spent at the office while his family stayed home because the business was in trouble and there was no money for a trip to the lake; it is the humiliation of taking all the insults a ruthless customer heaped on him and which he took because he needed the business; it is the endless hours of work with an employee to make him a good salesman and the frustration of having a big company hire him away because the small business could not afford a comparable pay scale; it is also the triumphant trip down to the bank to pay off that five-year loan after only three years; it is the near total satisfaction of having the small business prosper and grow to a point where someone makes a substantial offer to buy it out; it is all these things and many more that describe the business we call small, and the man or men who operate it whom we call small businessmen.

It is when such men have labored at their small business and have achieved some success that they most usually find a company or group of private investors to put up the funds required to finance their future growth. Such an association is usually required because the small businessman himself has more than likely already put up all his money to get his business that far.

In this book I have tried to describe small business in terms of some of the characteristics required of the small businessman himself, of some of the considerations important in getting a loan, in picking products or services, in making them and in organizing and managing—all with the emphasis on special considerations which must be made because of small size.

There is one further and last consideration that will come before every small businessman if he has aspirations of making his enterprise into more than a livelihood for himself. In

The Philosophy of a Venture Capitalist

this connection, I have never heard of, nor do I know of, a small business that has grown to any meaningful size where the small business man did not successfully accomplish this task. I refer to *picking a partner*.

I do not mean partner in the sense of an employee to share the management responsibilities. I mean a partner that will be a part owner in the business, who will provide guidance towards the acquisition, as needed, of the capital required to support the business growth. When the small businessman makes this connection, he will have picked a partner that will be with him from then on.

It has often seemed to me that this process was something akin to getting married. The similarity is in the final selection criteria. A man will pick his partner because he feels right about it. Hopefully, the other criteria have also been examined and the unacceptable candidates weeded out.

I call it a partnership because when a small businessman needs a lot of capital he will have to give the investor a *piece of the action*, as it is called. He will be required, in one way or another, to provide his investors with the opportunity for capital appreciation. They will be part owners of the business, and what they are looking for is profits—pure, simple profits.

I can assure every small businessman who has built his business to the point where he needs such help as these investors can provide, that there are as many different philosophies as to how such profits can be made as there are groups of investors. The small businessman had better pick as his partners a firm that appears to be looking for investments in business similar to the one into which he hopes he can build his own. If he does not, if he picks a firm that has different ideas about his business, then he will find himself with a partner that is holding him back and trying all the time to change him. Not only is this disconcerting and unpleasant, but such investors usually have the means of controlling and directing the business through their importance

The Philosophy of a Venture Capitalist

in the capital structure of the business and their control over financial arrangements.

There are all types of enterprises that are in the business of being this type of partner to small business. They are most frequently referred to as venture capital companies for the reason that they venture (or wager or invest) their stockholders' capital in small business. The *small business* part is important. I do not think a company which invested in big business would ever be called a venture capital company. It is usually called an investment banking company. Thus, the word venture is applied mainly to capital invested in *small* business.

The distinction is well made. There are no more or no less risks in small business than in big business. The difference is in the effect of the results of an unsuccessful risk. Every enterprise takes risks, but a small company may have to close its doors for a risk taken unsuccessfully while a business the size of Ford Motor Company can sustain a whopper the size of the Edsel.

On the other hand, the rewards of a risk taken successfully favor the small business. A small business that makes it into the big-time will see the original capital increase perhaps 1000 times, sometimes 5000 times, over a relatively short period. Thus, while an investment in General Motors offers a growth possibility of no mean proportion, it cannot compare with the capital growth in a successful small business.

That is why there are companies such as the venture capitalists. They exist for the purpose of providing a source of capital for the small business. And when a small business has grown to the point where it will be of interest to such a group, it will have entered the stage of its growth which precedes the state of being a big business.

It is at this point that the small businessman must make some fine distinctions. He must make his selection of the venture capital group on an informed basis if he is to live in harmony and make progress with them. Whether the small

The Philosophy of a Venture Capitalist

business becomes a big business or not depends to a large extent on how well the small business and the venture capital firm are matched.

What things should the small businessman be mindful of when picking his partners? I offer the following basic listing of the most important of these considerations:

Be sure the venture capital firm itself is making money and has a history as a money-maker.

There is an old saying that when money gets nervous it runs for the bank. What is meant by this is that a nervous investor will try to get his money out of a venture at the slightest sign of stormy seas ahead. Such investors will not be willing to stand behind their commitments in times of trouble.

A venture capital firm that has a history of making profits has undoubtedly had difficulties in the past and has met them successfully. There is only one thing an investor knows for certain, and that is that there will be trouble of some kind in every investment he makes. His determination to see his investments through their difficult times will be reflected in his own earnings statement.

The reason why this is so is very simple. The nervous investor who picks up and runs at the sound of trouble is almost always content to take a loss of some kind in order to extricate himself. The sum total of these losses will reflect itself in his own financial report. The nervous investors are the losers in the venture capital game. They stay in it because they somehow have the idea that they can make their money work for them. They do not know that making the investment should be the first and easiest work they will undertake with their small business client.

There is another most important consideration here. Many venture capital firms have a habit of making money for themselves, but the small businesses in which they have invested somehow don't seem to make out quite so well. It is always very interesting, therefore, to learn how the profits of

[147]

The Philosophy of a Venture Capitalist

the small businesses compare to the profits of the venture capital firm that has financed them. I will have more to say on this point later on.

Be sure the venture capital firm has the staff to work with your small business and that their investment is such that it is profitable for them to do so.

Contrary to what the nervous money people think, money will not work by itself. In an earlier chapter I likened money to the fertilizer that makes a garden grow and the oil that lubricates a machine. Money requires that some type of work be applied for its use to be in any way meaningful.

The venture capital firm should have the facilities at its disposal, usually in the form of personnel, to provide such help and do such work as the small business may require. The firm probably will not be able to provide these services unless the firm itself is profitable and unless its investment in the small business represents a profit-making opportunity.

These are the people who have an enlightened self-interest in the success of the small business in which they have invested. The small businessman can feel perfectly justified in calling on his investors whenever he needs them. If he has picked them well, they will have the special skills at hand that will be most helpful, or they will be prepared to obtain them. Also, they will believe they can improve their own profits in this way. More about this, too, later on.

Pick a partner who has the resources to go all the way with your company. Be sure the investor has enough funds available to provide the additional money that may be needed to help you through trouble and to carry your program to completion.

In an earlier chapter I made a few remarks about this same subject, and told the story of the man who borrowed from a group that later disbanded and left him high and dry. The same is true when taking in an investor, only more so. Whereas the lending group was providing funds for opera-

The Philosophy of a Venture Capitalist

tions, an investor will have bought stock and will be a partner in every sense of the word.

When a small businessman takes this step with a group he believes may not be able to see him all the way through his program and which might not be able to come up with additional investment funds as needed, he has done the same thing as if he had built a new plant that he knew would produce only part of what he required. There might be circumstances under which such a step would be justified, but they would have to be the result of a compromise. Particularly in the area of investment-type capital, obtaining less than the amount required to do the job may very well be worse for the small business than never having had access to the money in the first place.

This is well documented by the histories of many of the small businesses that went public during the boom in the new issues market of 1961 and '62. One case is illustrative of the dangers of being started on a program only to run out of funds later on. The case also indicates the very high cost of changing investment partners before the job has been completed.

The company was established, having been founded in 1950. It was engaged in the manufacture of industrial products that required a high degree of engineering. Much lead time was also required in the orderly acquisition of subcomponent parts. The items were bulky and heavy and much equipment and plant space was needed for the fabrication of the finished products.

This small business faced many of the problems that are typically found where an industry is controlled by five or six large companies. However, by frugality and hard work and because he was possessed of an inordinate engineering ability, the president of this small business had shown profits in almost every year.

Then one day he was visited by a man from one of the

The Philosophy of a Venture Capitalist

small underwriters. The proposition they had worked out was to provide the company with $250,000 of equity capital. This would purchase a one-half interest in the business, leaving the president with the other half. At the time, the company had a net worth of just under $100,000 and post-tax profits for the previous three years had averaged about $25,000 per year.

In other words, the underwriter proposed to sell 50 per cent of the common stock of the company to the public at large for a price of $250,000. This had the effect of placing a value on the entire company of $500,000. The president readily agreed to the proposal without making anything but the most cursory examination and check on the quality of the underwriters.

That was five years ago. The company is still paying for that underwriting and the costs are so great it is difficult to calculate them. The major costs have been:

For legal and accounting	
Attributable only to the underwriting	$25,000
Commissions to the underwriter	
In cash	$25,000
In stock	10,000
Annual estimated costs	
Attributable only to having publically traded stock—$6,000/year for five years	30,000
Total	$90,000

Thus, the company received a net amount of high cash of $190,000 from the underwriting, and expenses since then have further reduced this to $160,000 net cash received.

Against this the company has been able to earn an average of $35,000 per year after taxes. This is an increase of approximately $10,000 over the average earnings prior to the underwriting. Thus, the company has been able to show an estimated increase in net retained earnings of $50,000 over the

The Philosophy of a Venture Capitalist

five years which, for the purposes of illustrating this aspect of equity financing, can be assumed to be the result of the employment of the $160,000 cash. This is a return of about one-third over a five-year period, or about 6 per cent per year. While this could certainly be better, it is at least admissible as a net return on invested capital.

But the cost to the president has been fantastically high. He has, in effect, sold to others half of his business. The business, not the president, got the proceeds. With these proceeds, the business has not doubled in value as it would have had to in order for the president's remaining one-half ownership to be valued equally with his prior 100 per cent ownership.

The business has not doubled in value, and the explanation of why it did not is what happened after the underwriting. With the proceeds, the company moved its plant and offices to another location and acquired another company in closely related lines. At this point the president went back to his underwriter (investors) and demonstrated the need for more money to exploit the new set-up.

Not only was the general condition of the stock market completely changed by that time, making the raising of more capital next to impossible anyway, but the underwriter himself had gone out of business when the market collapsed in the fall of 1962. The company could not get any more money. And with the job only half done, the problem was very severe.

At this point, my own company became associated with this manufacturer. We supplied debt financing sufficient to carry the company through. *But,* we required some equity, and it will eventually be necessary for the company to again go to the capital market to get the cash to pay off the loans.

I believe the end result will be that the president will have to further dilute his percentage of ownership one-half again. Therefore, the conclusion will be that the president will own one-fourth of this company.

The Philosophy of a Venture Capitalist

The reasoning is that this one-fourth will be worth more than 100 per cent of what the company was worth before the first underwriting. While this might be true, the president *could have saved himself a minimum of one-fourth of his company* if he had been able to carry through with only one equity investor.

The point is clear. Each time a new group is brought in there is further dilution in the percentage of ownership. In the case I have just described, the first group could not be looked to for the entire amount of funds required. That is why I say the small businessman should pick as his equity investor a firm that will be able to stay with him, thereby avoiding *as much as possible* dilution of percentage of ownership of the original principals of the business.

This is, then, the first point in my philosophy of venture capitalism. The small businessman should not give up stock ownership of his business. Stock ownership should be his most valuable asset, and, if not valuable, at least it should be the one thing he owns that in a material sense he most cherishes.

I have often been criticized by my peers in the venture capital business for my view on this matter. They believe in getting all the stock ownership they can. My approach is the opposite. I try to figure the least amount of stock I am entitled to as compensation for the risks to which the investment I make will be exposed. Thus, when it comes to the point in the negotiations where everything is settled and the question is asked, "How much stock do you require?" I generally reply with another question by asking the small businessman what he thinks the risks really amount to and what would be the profit to which I would be entitled on that basis.

There is usually very little disagreement at this point. The small businessman has, by then, pretty well established the risks in his own mind and I have also made an estimate. It is surprising how close the two estimates usually come. It is

The Philosophy of a Venture Capitalist

only logical that this should be so if both of us have clearly analyzed the proposal. If the estimates are far apart and cannot be reconciled, then one of us has the wrong view—or perhaps we are both wrong. In this event, I would not go further, on the theory that such a basic disagreement at the start can only lead to one of us being unhappy with the deal—a condition that inevitably leads to trouble.

The second point of my philosophy is related to the first. Since I believe the small businessman should be allowed to keep the largest percentage of stock ownership, I try always to limit the risk as much as possible. This puts my company in the position of being entitled to only a smaller part of the ownership. It also serves the purpose of limiting the over-all risk ingredient to my company, which has the side advantage to the small businessman of providing stability to the company with which he has become a partner.

My understanding of the small businessman, and my experiences when I was one myself, have led me even further. I believe, as a matter of principle, that the small businessman should be the largest beneficiary of his own efforts. On occasion this belief has led me to turn down deals that I might otherwise have been inclined to make.

One time, especially, comes to mind. It was a successful chain of discount stores. Everything about the deal made sense. My analysis indicated there was some risk involved that could not be covered and I believed the equity investor in the situation was entitled to one-quarter of the profits and one-quarter of the stock ownership. The four principals did not disagree with me. If I had made the deal, however, my company would have been the single largest beneficiary; the principals would split the remainder between them, giving each a share that was smaller than mine.

It is possible that I was wrong in turning the deal down. The principals went elsewhere and got the equity money they needed. I understand they gave up 30 per cent stock ownership to the investing firm. So far, I understand, the program is working well. But I have seen deals like this go wrong so often that it may be too early to say I wasn't right.

What happens usually goes something like this. The small businessman has gotten his equity investors into his company. The investor firm now owns 60 per cent of his company—or, to put it another way, the small businessman has a remaining interest of 40 per cent. It is the middle of July, and hot and sticky with humidity, and some crazy driver bumped his car on the way to work. It is Sunday and his family at home didn't get any summer trip because he has been working on a business deal that has required all his time. Profits have been hurt as a result of putting up the new equipment to handle the proposed deal. As a result, the small businessman has not yet paid himself for June in an effort to conserve company cash. Thus, the family cannot afford even a long weekend trip. While he is at the plant, something else happens; his production manager calls up to say he won't be in to help him as promised, and, as a matter of fact, is going to quit anyway.

At this point, the small businessman may very well decide to quit fighting; he may reason that he is going to make his investors richer than himself and to hell with it all. You must believe me that it has happened just this way many times. The small businessman will quit fighting, although he probably won't tell anybody he has. From then on the push isn't there anymore, the drive and desire have been dissipated and the small business will certainly not do as well as it could have. It may even go downhill and eventually be lost.

I am determined that one of the factors that will cause a small businessman to give up will never be his association with my company. To that end, and under no circumstances, will I ever put my company in such a position that it owns more of a business than its founder.

Sometimes it is not at the first investment that many equity investors drive their hardest bargain. It may be when the small businessman comes back for the second round of money that they will ask for additional stock. This is, again, contrary to my philosophy. I always make my deal for stock at the time of the first investment. I make it as clear as I can that this is the *only* time we will talk about stock on the financing. If the small businessman needs more money because his company has prospered and grown as a result of the first financing, then I want him to come back to my company for the rest.

I certainly don't give my stockholders' money away on such occasions. Usually a long-term loan is added to the existing financing, and we charge interest on such loans. But the idea is that if the small businessman has done well with the first money, he has already improved the value of whatever stock we took the first time, and that is sufficient additional compensation over and above the interest.

Of course, if there have been losses, or if the small businessman is proposing to take on something entirely new, then I will review the proposal to see if there are new risk ingredients present and, if so, try to cover them.

There is one more very important tenet in my philosophy. It is that the small businessman should be the one to give me my profit on any stock I might hold in his company. To this end I will arrange, in advance, for the method of calculation of what his price will be. I work it out with the small businessman so that my company makes a profit and he gets a good buy on his own stock. Most small businessmen very much appreciate the knowledge they can buy me out if they want to.

It is, after all, the man's own business. It should always remain that way so long as the small businessman wants it to. If he changes his mind and wants to go for broke, that also is perfectly acceptable, and I will stay with him all the way.

My philosophy is a very simple one. I believe that a man is trying to do a great many things when he undertakes to build a small business. All the venture capitalist does is provide money, guidance and encouragement; the small

The Philosophy of a Venture Capitalist

businessman provides the toil, heartache, drive and vision. Above all else, the ownership of his enterprise should remain under his control and he should be the largest beneficiary of his success. Having achieved the success he wants, he should not be forced to go further. At that time he should be provided with the means of getting back the ownership of his company at a cost to himself he can afford and that will provide a profit for his partners. The venture capitalist must be content with the smaller profit thus negotiated. Or if the small businessman has dreams of building an empire, then again the equity investors must be prepared to go along.

There is one type of venture capital firm that operates on the basis that one big winner will make up for a number of losers. For this philosophy to work a large equity appreciation must be obtained in each small business so that when there is a winner the profits are large. In my view, that is a busted philosophy that will end in ruin for the very simple reason that I do not think a small businessman has any interest in making someone else wealthier than himself.

I believe in a slower more stable growth for my own company and for the companies in which I have invested my stockholders' money. I am perfectly content to have a number of small business clients that are making modest and stable profits and that will, hopefully, be able to repay the loans I have made them and provide my company with a reasonable—probably small—profit.

There is nothing more pleasant to contemplate than a profitable, growing small business. I want to be a junior partner in all I can get.

About the Author

Louis L. Allen was born in Cincinnati, Ohio, in 1925. After three years in the Armed Forces in Europe during World War II, in which he saw combat as a rifleman in the Infantry, he attended Harvard University, where he received an A.B. Degree in 1950 and a Masters Degree in Business Administration in 1952.

His career since then has been exclusively in small business. He has been the proprietor of his own business, an officer in several small manufacturing companies, and a partner and consultant in several other small business ventures. For several years he was active in education for small businessmen in Cleveland at Case Institute of Technology, and for five years was chief operating officer of the First Small Business Investment Corporation of New Jersey, one of the country's leading publicly held SBICs.

Mr. Allen has been a guest lecturer at various universities, including Harvard, Rutgers, and New York University, and has written about the problems of small business for several journals. While he was associated with the American Management Association he developed the small business courses and seminars which are still a popular feature of that organization's program. In 1954 Mr. Allen, along with some 20 other men, was a founder of the National Association for Small Business Management Development, an organization that has grown to important size and at present represents a cross-section of both educators and practitioners of small business throughout the country.

The small business investment company of which Mr. Allen is the president is the small business arm of the Chase Manhattan Bank, N.A., one of the world's leading banks.